MINDY MEIER

Sex and Dating

Questions You Wish You Had Answers To

IVP Books

An imprint of InterVarsity Press
Downers Grove, Illinois

InterVarsity Press
P.O. Box 1400, Downers Grove, IL 60515-1426
World Wide Web: www.ivpress.com
E-mail: email@ivpress.com

InterVarsity Press® is the book-publishing division of InterVarsity Christian Fellowship/USA®, a movement of students and faculty active on campus at hundreds of universities, colleges and schools of nursing in the United States of America, and a member movement of the International Fellowship of Evangelical Students. For information about local and regional activities, write Public Relations Dept., InterVarsity Christian Fellowship/USA, 6400 Schroeder Rd., P.O. Box 7895, Madison, WI 53707-7895, or visit the IVCF website at <www.intervarsity.org>.

All Scripture quotations, unless otherwise indicated, are taken from the Holy Bible, Today's New International Version™ *Copyright © 2001 by International Bible Society. All rights reserved.*

Material on pp. 122-24 from Three Kinds of Love *by Masumi Toyotome is used with permission of InterVarsity Press, © 1961 by Masumi Toyotome.*

All the accounts in this book are real stories of real people, but names and some identifying details have been changed to protect the privacy of the the individuals. Some stories are composites of multiple people.

Every effort has been made to trace and contact copyright holders for additional materials quoted in this book. The author will be pleased to rectify any omissions in future editions if notified by copyright holders.

Design: Cindy Kiple
Images: Todd Korol/Getty Images

ISBN 978-0-8308-3605-5

Printed in the United States of America ∞

Library of Congress Cataloging-in-Publication Data

Meier, Mindy, 1950-
    Sex and dating: questions you wish you had answers to / Mindy
Meier.
        p. cm.
    Includes bibliographical references.
    ISBN-13: 978-0-8308-3605-5 (pbk.: alk. paper)
1. Sex—Religious aspects—Christianity. 2. Dating (Social
customs)—Religious aspects—Christianity. I. Title.
BT708.M4352007
241'.66—dc22

                                                                              2007031453

| **P** | 24 | 23 | 22 | 21 | 20 | 19 | 18 | 17 | 16 | 15 | 14 | 13 | 12 | 11 | 10 | 9 |
| **Y** | 29 | 28 | 27 | 26 | 25 | 24 | 23 | 22 | 21 | 20 | 19 | 18 | 17 | 16 | 15 | |

This book is dedicated to Bill Meier—

my husband, best friend and partner in pleasure.

And to our children—

Tiffany and her husband, Will O'Brien,

Meredith and her husband, Randy Nonnenberg,

Luke and

Rob

Contents

Introduction

I get a lot of questions about sex.

Sex dominates our society. Turn on a radio or TV or pick up a magazine and there's a good chance the theme is sex, dating or romantic relationships. But while sex and relationships are often our most pressing and confusing concerns, sometimes it's hard to know where to voice them. It takes a lot of trust to bring these topics up.

During my twenty years of spiritually mentoring college students, I've had the privilege of getting to know many young people who, somewhere along the line, came to trust me enough to bring up their most intimate concerns. Perhaps in the overwhelming university atmosphere, it's easier to talk to someone older and neutral. Whatever the reason, I have listened to hundreds of stories and have sought to impart my best advice about sex and dating.

People come to me seeking guidance and wisdom, but the paradox is they have in fact been my teachers. As people have shared their stories and revealed their heartaches, joys and deepest dreams, they've taught me much about the complicated journey of pursuing love and coming to terms with one's sexuality. I consider each story a sacred trust.

So what business does someone my age have writing a book about sex? I like to think that living on a college campus and spending the bulk of my time with university students has kept me informed. Times and trends change, but the issues are often the same. Getting upset by something on your boyfriend's MySpace profile is a new problem, but jealousy is as old as time.

God could have made sex a much more boring enterprise. He could have made us void of desire for romantic relationships. But somehow in God's good wisdom, he chose to make us male and female with deep longings to connect. God thought up sex, his wonderful gift to people. God hard-wired us for relationships and built into us sexual desires, but we are imperfect people living in an imperfect world. Sometimes we need help figuring things out.

The content of this book is presented in a Q & A format. It has grown out of questions that real people have asked me over the years on the topics of sex and dating. These questions come up over and over again in coffee shops, during student appointments, seminars and e-mails. Some of these questions will be of interest to you; others won't. Feel free to skip around and read the ones that intersect with your life. There's no need to read everything in order. I know how busy life can be, so my hope is that the format will help you zero in on the areas of concern to you.

By using a Q & A format, I don't mean to suggest that these are questions with one clear, simple answer. People are too complex to have one answer suffice for all situations. I honestly wish I could sit down with you personally, over a decaf skim latte (with extra whipped cream) and hear your specific story and enter into your heart. I have had the luxury of doing things this way often, but sadly a book won't allow it. And so I have done my best to supply general answers to the questions presented. My hope is that you'll see your story in the stories of the people I have written about.

It feels a bit awkward to write on an area in which we all feel insecure and have suffered failures. Don't think that I have figured out everything, and don't assume I no longer struggle with any of the issues discussed. I do. Like you, I'm an imperfect human being trying to navigate my way through life and love.

I'm not an expert, but I've spent years listening—not only as a campus minister but also as a pastor's wife. Being with people through different life stages from the cradle to the grave has been instructive. So has raising my four kids, all in their twenties now (two married and two single), who have confided in me as they found their way through today's dating world.

All of these rich life experiences have taught me a great deal about this area of our lives that touches us so deeply but often leaves us so confused. I'm happy that some of the knowledge people imparted to me will find its way to others. I'm forever grateful to them for their trust and vulnerability.

By the way, all the accounts in this book are real stories of real people, but I have changed names and some identifying details to protect their privacy. Some stories are composites of multiple people.

I want you to know that even in a world of short-term relationships and hookups, *lifelong love is possible*. My husband, Bill, and I are proof of that. We have been married over thirty years, and the process of interweaving our lives has been joyous, turbulent, fulfilling, and frankly, difficult at times. But through it all, we have confronted our own brokenness and deepened in our love and understanding of one another.

I write this book as a Christian. I have become convinced of God's reality and relevance in my life, and I've seen the power of Jesus transform lives and heal pain and sexual brokenness. I'm also convinced of the value and wisdom in God's written Word, the Bible, which has much to say about sexuality and relationships. But whether you're a Christian or not, whether you're sexually active or not, whether you're in a serious relationship or have never dated, I hope this book helps you move toward healthy relationships.

PART ONE

Sex

1 Is there more to sex than pleasure?

Nearly all of us long for relationships. We're drawn toward others for completion. Most of us long to connect with another person and to share experiences that bond us mind, body and soul. The reason we have this universal longing is because God designed us this way. He also created us with sexual desires. He imprinted on our bodies and souls the longing for consummation. Sex is one of God's most wonderful gifts to human beings.

In the fall of 2005, the incoming freshman class at the University of Illinois was asked, "What do you want most out of your college career?" For the first time, the top answer was to someday have a family, ahead of options such as to earn a degree that will ensure a good income and to develop a philosophy of life. This finding came as a surprise to many of the university's administrators. In an institution that prides itself on academic excellence, this hunger for family seemed incongruous.

Of course there are people who don't have these desires. If their parents' marriage was a source of pain or ended in divorce, these longings may not be present. Some folks so value their independence that bonding with one person sounds limiting. But most people, deep down inside, want to someday have a loving and deeply connected marriage.

An important part of marriage is sex. What happens when two people unite through sexual intercourse? What's the purpose of sex?

SEVEN PURPOSES OF SEX

Perhaps the first purpose of sex that we think of is *pleasure*. We experience exhilarating pleasure as we fully share our body with another. God made people with body parts designed for sexual pleasure. Some parts of our body have no function other than sexual pleasure. By design, we are pleasure givers and pleasure receivers. If you think Christians and the church are antisex and antipleasure, it's worth noting that an entire book of the Bible, the Song of Songs, is devoted to the romantic, sensual love between a man and a woman.

The two lovers in the Song of Songs use metaphors to express the sensual delights of physical love. He invites her to come and experience the sights and smells of spring: "Arise my darling, my beautiful one, come with me. See! The winter is past; the rains are over and gone. Flowers appear on the earth; the season of singing has come, the cooing of doves is heard in our land. The fig tree forms its early fruit; the blossoming vines spread their fragrance. Arise, come, my darling; my beautiful one, come with me" (Song of Songs 2:10-13). In this text we see love's invitation to be a partner in pleasure.

A husband and wife are partners in pleasure. Sex is part of that, but so is watching the sun set together or tearing into a loaf of hot bread from the oven or walking barefoot on the beach or lying in the hammock admiring the paint job you worked on together on the deck. Rich or poor, educated or uneducated, beautiful or ordinary, all married couples can enjoy the wonders and delights of sexual love. It takes a lifetime to plumb the depths of sexual love in a marriage.

Another purpose for sex is *bonding*. The act of sexual intercourse is intended by God to act as superglue in the relationship, bonding two people together. We become attached to someone when we experience physical touch and pleasure in a loving way. Sex is so much more than the joining of body parts. Sex unites souls.

In Genesis 4:1 (ESV), we read, "Adam knew Eve his wife, and she conceived and bore Cain." The first time I read this, I figured the writer cut out the spicy stuff to make the Bible PG-13. But *to know* is a rich word in Hebrew that means to deeply know in a full and total way. Adam knew her sexually but also emotionally and spiritually. To have sexual intercourse is to share a secret, and the secret bonds the partners together.

An additional purpose for sex is *the creation of new life.* Sexual intercourse sometimes results in pregnancy. In the context of this loving union, a place is made to bring new life into the world. The overflow of the love a man and woman have for one another spills out and pours into the life of a baby.

The first command God gave people is found in Genesis 1:28, "God blessed them and said to them, 'Be fruitful and increase in number; fill the earth and subdue it.'" God restated this to Noah and his family after the flood. This is the only command in the Bible that we have done well at following. Children are a gift from God, to be received with joy, awe and thanksgiving. Psalm 127:3 says, "Children are a heritage from the LORD, offspring a reward from him." Children are intended by God to be one of life's greatest blessings.

Fourth is *communication.* Sexual intercourse is a wordless way of saying, "I love you; I'm giving myself to you." It's a deeper-than-words message, a beyond-words way to communicate with another. As we channel our passion to the other, we celebrate who they are and our delight to be in union with them. To be naked with a marriage partner is a wordless declaration of honesty, trust and self-giving.

A fifth purpose for sex is *transformation* from being self-absorbed to being other-centered. Sex pulls us out of our self-absorption to unite us with another human being. Jesus gives an indication of this unity when he says, "The two will become one flesh" (Mark 10:8). Marriage is a laboratory to learn how to love. Philip Yancey writes, "I went into marriage thinking love would hold us together. I learned instead that it required marriage to teach me what love means."[1] Sexual love allows us to practice mutual submission where the desires and pleasure of another become as important to us as our own.

A sixth purpose is *emotional release*. The sexual experience provides an outlet to pour out pent-up emotions. In the union between a husband and wife, when they reach orgasms (either at the same time or different times) tension that has been building finds satisfaction.

And finally sex is a *reflection of our desire for God*. In *Sexuality and Holy Longing*, Lisa McMinn says, "Sex is a spiritual metaphor for our consummate longing for God. It is an act that can draw our hearts toward God, in whom all our longings will one day be met. . . . Sex can still be an act God uses to pursue our hearts. All longings go unfulfilled this side of heaven. In our experience of sexuality, whether within marriage or without, we ultimately recognize that what we long for won't be experienced this side of heaven."[2]

Because the body and soul are one, when we have sexual intercourse with someone and they touch our body, they also touch our soul. Sexual intercourse is so much more than skin touching skin.

RETHINKING SEX

Sex has often been likened to fire. Fire is wonderful if it's in the fireplace or the furnace to keep us warm or if it's used for cooking, but fire can also be destructive. When flames are out of control your house can burn to the ground. Fire is only good or useful when used in the right context. It's the same with sex.

Because of the great power of sex—to be either a source of unspeakable joy and ecstasy or a source of deep pain and sorrow—God has laid out some restrictions for us. These rules are not imposed to spoil our fun and pleasure but rather to protect something of great value. God wants the best for us. He designed us and knows how we are wired. He wants to protect us from emotional pain and sexually transmitted diseases.

Think for a moment about your first impression of sex. What did you pick up from TV, magazines and movies? What attitude did your parents convey? Was sex presented as a necessary evil, something to be joked about, a dirty thing to be ashamed of, a precious gift from God to be saved for marriage? Many people say that sex was presented only as something people do to conceive children, and other than that, sex was considered a bad thing. You may have never talked with your parents about sex, but parents can convey attitudes and feelings without words. To never talk about sex also conveys a message.

What messages did you pick up from kids on the playground? Chances are that know-it-all fifth-grade boy was full of misinformation. This is worth thinking about because you may need to consciously reject some of the erroneous ideas you were fed. Warped views of sex have a way of persisting even when we know in our head that they are wrong.

As a kid, I always peppered my mom with questions. When I was about eight years old, I asked my mom a bunch of questions about where babies came from. I was persistent and pressed her to know exactly how babies got inside their mothers' tummies. My mom told me about sexual intercourse. She was open, honest and matter of fact about it. My response was, "Oh, that's gross! I'll never do that!" She laughed softly and said, "When I was your age, I felt the same way, but when you're older and married and in love with a man, you'll think it's wonderful." That powerful statement shaped my view of sex. It stuck with me and became the foundation of my view of sex.

Fast-forward about a decade. I was a teenager, and my parents were going away for the weekend—just the two of them. While my mom packed, she gave me instructions for the weekend, when to pick my sister up from her ballet lesson and so on. As I listened to her litany of directives, I noticed she was packing a sexy black negligee. At first I thought, *Was she going to wear that with Dad?* But then I thought, *Wow, that's awesome that they still have these romantic getaways together even though they're so old!* This was another formative event that shaped my view of sex in marriage.

Do you need to rethink your view of sex? My hope is that you'll catch a glimpse of God's wonderful view of sex and that it will capture your heart and transform the way you live.

This is what happened to Maria. I ran into her at the wedding of a mutual friend. We hadn't seen one another in seven years. The slow-moving buffet line gave us ample time to catch up.

Maria had been a party girl in college and had slept around, always hoping that her current boyfriend would be the lasting love of her life. Serial lovers left her feeling broken and confused. But when she became a Christian at the end of her senior year of college, she began to reclaim a vision for purity and committed herself to chastity. After graduation, she took a job where she eventually met her husband, Juan. He was a committed Christian as well.

As we waited our turn to load up our plates, Maria said, "You know, the sex I have with my husband now is way better than all the sex I had in college. That sex was destructive. It left me feeling empty. But sex within marriage builds me up. When I look at my adorable kids, I wish I could go back and tell my younger self, 'Don't sleep around. It only messes you up. Have sex the way God intends—in marriage.'"

For the first time in my life I was glad for a slow-moving food line. It gave me a chance to hear Maria's heart and see the beauty of her life.

2 Is it wrong to have sex outside of marriage if we love each other?

Drew began dating Amy at the beginning of his junior year. Growing up in a home with little affirmation, Drew was immediately drawn in by Amy's warmth and ready smile. Knowing that grad school lay ahead and that neither set of parents would foot the bill for school if they were married, they put marriage on the back burner. Their emotional and physical intimacy deepened, and they began having sex on a regular basis. This gave them pangs of guilt when they went to church. They justified their situation by saying, "We plan to get married someday, so why not enjoy sex now? What difference does a piece of paper make?"

How should Drew's and Amy's faith affect their view of sex? The Bible presents sex as a wonderful gift to be enjoyed by married people, but because of the powerful nature of sex, the Bible also establishes boundaries for it. The Bible uses several different words for sexual sin. One word is *adultery*, which is used when a married person has sex with someone other than his or her marriage partner. One of the Ten Commandments is, "You shall not commit adultery" (Exodus 20:14). Jesus affirmed this command in Mark 10:19 when he said, "You know the commandments: 'You shall not murder, you shall not commit adultery, you shall not steal, you shall not give false testimony, you shall not defraud, honor your father and mother.'"

A different word is used for sexual immorality between two unmarried people: *porneia* in the original language of the New Testament. Some older Bibles translate this as *fornication*. Newer Bibles translate the same word as *sexual immorality*. This word is found in 1 Thessalonians 4:3-6: "It is God's will that you should be sanctified [set apart as holy]: that you should avoid sexual immorality *[porneia]*; that each of you should learn to control your own body in a way that is holy and honorable, not in passionate lust like the pagans, who do not know God; and that in this matter no one should wrong or take advantage of a brother or sister."

This text contains some wonderful lessons. It begins with the overarching principle that it's God's will for us to be sanctified or set apart as holy. Our bodies and our sexual passions should be given over to God for his purposes.

The idea inherent in the clause, "You should avoid sexual immorality," isn't keeping sexual immorality to a minimum. Rather it's an exhortation to take radical steps to avoid falling into sexual sin. In other words, think of situations that might set you up to fall into sexual sin and avoid those situations.

The text also says we aren't to be consumed by lust like those who don't know God.

And the last sentence, "no one should wrong or take advantage of a brother or sister," uses the marketplace word *pleonekteo* that refers to someone being ripped off. When you have sex with someone you're not married to, you're stealing from that person's future marriage partner and your future marriage partner. If neither of you marries in the future, then what was meant to be set aside for God's purposes is given away.

TRUST THE MAKER

The teaching of Scripture is clear, but can we trust God? Does he really know us and have our best interests in mind? The answers to these questions are illustrated in *True Love in a World of False Hope* by Robbie Castleman:

A young man in the early days of automobiles was having trouble with his Model T Ford. The car was on the side of an old dirt road, and no matter what the young man did, it wouldn't start. An elderly man with a cane and slow walk came along and offered to help. The young man politely declined the old guy's offer with an attitude of "thanks, but no thanks." The older fellow shook his head, mentioned what he thought the problem was from the sounds the car made, and began to pass on his way. He stopped after going just a short distance and called back some advice on how to get the car started.

The young man thought to himself, "What can this old guy know about fixing a car? He's probably never even ridden in one." He tinkered for a few minutes, kicked the tires, cursed and then tried what the man had suggested. He was amazed when the car started right up! He drove off down the road and overtook the old man as he continued his walk. With a new respect, he thanked the man for his advice and then asked him, "So when did you come to know so much about cars?"

And the old guy smiled and said matter-of-factly, "Well, son, my name is Henry Ford, and I made that car."[3]

In the same way Henry Ford knows what's best for the car, our Creator knows what's best for us. God has given us the Bible, rich with instruction on how to live. We must always remember that God's restrictions for us grow out of his protective love. He knows us better than we know ourselves.

When my son Rob was small, he always wanted to play in the street because the ball bounced better there and there was more room. My hard and fast rule, no playing in the street, seemed so restrictive, yet it grew out of my love for him. I knew that playing in the street put him at risk for being hit by a car, but it's hard to convince an athletic five-year-old boy of the dangers. In the same way, God's restrictions for us may seem to make no sense to us now, but we must trust that they are for our best.

Sexual intercourse was intended by God to be a bonding experience, knitting the souls of two people together. To unite with someone and then break up is damaging to the spirit and soul. It's like gluing two objects together and then pulling them apart. Damage occurs to both objects as you split them up. Similarly, great damage takes place when you unite in body and soul with another person and then go your separate ways. Often the degree of heartache experienced after a breakup is determined by the level of sexual intimacy shared in the relationship.

You never know for sure you'll marry someone until you walk back up the aisle after exchanging your wedding vows. Almost all married people thought they would marry someone else. I've often listened to gut-wrenching stories that included "I thought *for sure* we were getting married!" These people are dealing with the death of their dreams and often with deep regrets if they were sexually involved. Many people realize they've given away an irretrievable part of themselves.

Having sexual relations with numerous people gives you the raw material for comparison. Later, if you marry, you might compare your marriage partner with past lovers and past experiences. This is never helpful.

I know of one couple who divorced because of sexual comparisons. One of the death blows to their relationship came in a huge, uncontrolled argument after several years of marriage and two kids. The wife let her husband know that he wasn't as good in bed as her old boyfriend. He was utterly devastated.

WHEN THE RULES DON'T APPLY

What about couples who know God's standards but think they somehow are above them?

Several years ago, I was at a Christian conference leading a seminar on sexuality. Carrie, a junior in college, approached me to talk about her relationship with her boyfriend, Gabriel. She told me that she and Gabriel were both Christians and were having sexual intercourse. After talking with her for a while, I could see that they both knew the biblical passages that speak against sex outside of marriage, but Gabriel had convinced her that those texts did not apply to them.

I had never met Carrie before then and knew little about her or her boyfriend, but she had mentioned that he worked at a car dealership. I gave an illustration to explain my point. I said, "If Gabriel thinks he can sidestep God's laws on sex now, he'll be prone to do the same thing later in another area. Suppose the dealership Gabriel works for has a promotion that you get a free TV if you buy a car. Gabriel might steal a TV from the boss, justifying it by saying, 'He really underpays me, and so this TV is making up for the salary I should have received.'"

Carrie's face fell. She said, "Wow! That really did happen last week! He came home with a TV and said he took it from the boss, but he felt justified because he's so underpaid."

We were both a little freaked out that my random story had been so accurate, but it caused her to see the real danger of thinking God's standards are for other people, but not for her.

After talking with Carrie, I realized that for her the question of sex outside of marriage was a secondary question. The real question was, what role does God play in my life? Answering that question would direct her decision about continuing to have sex with her boyfriend.

Many people practice what I call "LEGO theology." They take

something they heard on Oprah, a line off a Hallmark greeting card, a verse from a plaque in their grandmother's kitchen or some poetry from a Zen Buddhist book and add some verse from the Bible. They craft their own personal designer religion. But are we free to do that? Our human inclination is to form views that accommodate our behavior. But we are wise only when we draw from the richness of our Christian faith communities and the timeless truth of Scripture.

If you're dating someone and engaging in sexual intercourse, don't completely despair. There is hope for you. Turn to God and ask him for forgiveness. First John 1:9 says, "If we confess our sins, he is faithful and just and will forgive us our sins and purify us from all unrighteousness." God has the ability to wash us clean and give us a new beginning.

God loves us so much that he gives us guidelines for living a full and joyous life. When we come to see his prohibitions as expressions of his care, we'll seek to obey them, knowing that blessing and wholeness follow. The quest to know God and follow his ways will shape our choices.

3 The person I'm dating wants me to set the boundaries. Is that okay?

I sat with Susan in the basement of the student union when she asked me this question: "David and I have been dating for several weeks now. He told me that he wants me to set the boundaries for our sexual involvement. He will go along with whatever boundaries I set for our relationship. Do you think this is okay?"

Both Susan and David were leaders in the campus Christian fellowship, and both honestly wanted to please God in this area of their lives. David's desire to set boundaries and talk about them was admirable. His desire for her to set the boundaries may have grown out of his desire to be nice and let her decide the pace of their relationship. I acknowledged these points, but the rest of my response surprised Susan. "Honestly, I think it's a bad idea for you to set the boundaries alone. If you set the boundaries and he goes along with them, you're forced to be the brains of the operation. You'll also have the role of enforcing the boundaries. That lets him off the hook. It undermines his opportunity to show you he's a man who has convictions and carries them out."

TRUST OR DISTRUST

What many people don't realize is that the dating relationship becomes the foundation of marriage. Imagine that Susan sets the boundaries, policing David's sex drive and her own. Ten years later when they are married and he takes a business trip to California, leaving Susan at home in Chicago, she will have fear. She'll be thinking, *I managed his sex drive when we were dating, but I won't be there in California to police him. What if some woman hits on him? Will he have the integrity and self-discipline to say no?* The answer to that question will come from the private moments Susan observed David during their dating relationship.

A man once came into my husband's office and said, "I'm afraid my wife will cheat on me."

My husband, Bill, asked, "Are you finding evidence of another guy in her life?"

He eventually said, "No, but you see when we were dating, my wife told me she didn't believe in premarital sex and wanted to wait until marriage. But I badgered her, I sweet-talked her, and I was able to talk her into doing something I knew she was opposed to doing. I wonder if some other guy could do that to her. In all honesty, I see her as pretty spineless."

What happens in the private moments of a dating relationship becomes the basis of trust or distrust later in the marriage. It's important that both people set their own boundaries and police themselves. Managing their own sex drives also provides the opportunity to develop character traits such as self-control and integrity that will be beneficial during marriage.

Some people find it difficult to carry out the boundaries they've set, not because of sexual passion, but because they melt into others' requests. For example, a woman said to me, "I feel horrible. Last weekend some friends came to visit me, and one guy stayed later than anyone else. It was getting late, and I wanted him to leave, but I didn't know how to get him to go. He started coming on to me, wanting to have sex. I really didn't want to at all, but I didn't know how to say no. I didn't want him to be upset, so I just gave in. It was horrible, but I couldn't figure out how to say no without offending him."

If you have found yourself giving in to sexual advances when you didn't want to, you may be helped by reading *Boundaries: When to Say Yes, When to Say No, to Take Control of Your Life.*[4] The book answers questions like these: Can I set limits and still be a loving person? Why do I feel guilty or afraid when I consider setting boundaries?

Two people who are dating may have differing opinions about where to set boundaries. If a woman has been raped or abused, she may flinch at even an arm around the shoulder. In that case, it may be caring and sensitive for the man to say, "I don't want to do anything that makes you feel uncomfortable. I want you to feel safe in my presence."

It makes sense for both people to set boundaries and then abide by the stricter boundaries. People shouldn't be forced to do something they don't feel comfortable with. One way we can show love for our partners is by respecting their boundaries even when we don't share their convictions.

4 How far can we go?

How far can we go? This question has a short answer and a long answer.

The short answer is this: Imagine for a moment that a person exists who you will one day marry. Imagine you have not yet met this person, but this person is going on a date tonight. What do you want your future marriage partner to do sexually with his or her date? Most people respond with a brief reflective look and then an impassioned "Nothing!" There's your short answer.

Now for the long answer. The overarching truth taught by the Bible and the Christian community is that sex was created by God to be enjoyed in the context of marriage. Proverbs 5:15-20 exhorts a married man to find sexual delight in his wife. The wife is likened to a refreshing source of water. Wells and springs were privately owned and of great value in the Middle East.

> "Drink water from your own cistern, running water from your own well. Should your springs overflow in the streets, your streams of water in the public squares? Let them be yours alone, never to be shared with strangers. May your fountain be blessed, and may you rejoice in the wife of your youth. A loving

doe, a graceful deer—may her breasts satisfy you always, may you ever be intoxicated with her love. Why, my son, be intoxicated with another man's wife? Why embrace the bosom of a wayward woman?"

In this text, the husband is exhorted to channel all of his passion toward his wife. The picture is one of ecstasy in the context of a monogamous marriage relationship.

If you're dating, realize you may not marry that person. It's common to date and not end up marrying that person, so it's always worth asking these questions:

- If we break up and marry other people will I have any regrets?
- Am I giving something away that should be saved for the person I marry?
- If we break up and marry other people, would it be weird running into him or her two years from now at the wedding of a mutual friend? (Trust me, this is a very common scenario.)

Rachel Safier, author of *There Goes the Bride* (which is a survival guide for broken engagements), estimates that 20 percent of engaged couples call it off before the wedding—about 500,000 people a year.[5] The truth is you don't know for sure who you'll marry until you recite your wedding vows.

THE EVERYTHING-BUT STRATEGY

Knowing that sexual intercourse outside of marriage is forbidden for Christians, many couples practice the everything-but strategy. When I was in college, my husband and I had dear friends who had dated for many years and wanted to save intercourse for after their wedding. However they followed the everything-but strategy during their dating years. They would passionately kiss and touch one another, but just before intercourse, they would slam on the brakes. They continued this practice for many months. But they did wait until their wedding day for intercourse.

After they had been married a number of months, the wife confided in me that she was unable to go on with the full expression of sexual intercourse. She said, "For so many years I trained myself to shut down, to turn off, to abort the operation just before intercourse, that now, even when I'm married and it's okay, I still cannot allow myself to naturally continue on in the act of intercourse. I just freeze up even when I don't want to."

In her mind she had compartmentalized foreplay as okay but intercourse as bad. Years of programming are hard to break out of. Foreplay is intended to prepare the body and soul for sexual intercourse. It's detrimental to become highly aroused and then slam on the brakes repeatedly.

Sexual pleasure is intended by God to be a source of joy, not guilt. Fusing the experience of sexual pleasure with guilt is damaging. Later in marriage it can be difficult to shake the notion that sex is bad.

I recommend that people spend time alone with God in prayer and reflection. Ask him to show you where your boundaries should be. It's important to have clear boundaries, even if you aren't in a dating relationship. Setting your personal guidelines when you're not dating is a more effective time to think this through than on a romantic moonlit night, in a foggy state of romance.

When I was in college, I heard a speaker that challenged us to set boundaries, and I drafted mine even though I wasn't dating anyone. I came up with four concrete guidelines that I could keep track of. I'm not legislating these for you. They're to help prompt your thinking. Please ask God to guide you. Here are my four:

1. Don't sleep overnight in the same bed. Couples often ask, "Is it okay to sleep together in the same bed even if nothing happens?" Upon further dialogue, it becomes apparent that things *are* happening, just not intercourse. But to lie next to someone is extremely tempting and puts people in a dangerous position where falling is likely.

Also, many married people rate falling asleep in the arms of the person they married as one of the top five great things about being married. It's too precious to be shared with multiple people.

2. Keep clothing on. Peeling off a sweatshirt over a T-shirt on a warm day is fine. I mean don't take off clothing that results in a loss of modesty.

3. Don't touch body parts that are covered by a two-piece swimsuit for women or swim trunks for men. All of our body parts are good and beautiful, but some are so precious that they are meant to be shared only with the marriage partner.

4. Don't lie on top of one another. It's one thing to lie on the couch to watch a TV show or on a blanket to enjoy an outdoor picnic. What I'm referring to is lying on top of one another in a way that simulates intercourse.

A number of engaged people have shared with me that they wish they had done less sexually, sometimes with a high school girlfriend or boyfriend, sometimes with the one they are about to marry. But no one has ever said they wish they had done more.

INEXPERIENCE HAS BENEFITS

Occasionally I talk to a Christian guy who has kept himself sexually pure and fears that his lack of sexual experience will be a liability when he gets married. Perhaps he has heard other guys boast of sexual exploits, which causes him to wonder if he should get some experience to know how to satisfy a woman.

I always assure these young men that their track record of self-control will make the women they marry deeply trust them. Women reason, "If he was sexually pure before he met me and was self-controlled in our dating relationship, then I know for sure he'll be faithful to me after we're married."

The feeling of being safe in a husband's love allows a woman to relax and give herself unreservedly to him; sexual pleasure is unleashed. A woman's sexual arousal has to do more with the quality of the relationship than with techniques. When I talk with married couples who are having trouble in their sex lives, they are often having problems with the way they treat each other and relate to each other. When sexual problems show up, they are not usually about sex.

Inexperience becomes a virtue when you realize that you're not being compared to a former lover. I'm sure that Adam and Eve had a great deal of fun figuring things out.

As you think about the dating relationship you *want*, also think about what you *will* do. Enjoy holding hands on long walks. Share your hearts in meaningful conversations. Learn a new sport or skill together. Take hikes and delight in creation. Visit an art gallery or attend a music concert. Practice hospitality as a couple. Care for the poor or help build a home through Habitat for Humanity. In healthy relationships, energy is directed outward to the service of others. Seek to discover what it means to follow Jesus with heart, soul, mind and strength as a couple.

RECLAIMING COURTSHIP

One of the things I would love to see reclaimed in today's dating culture is the delightful process of courtship. I'm not referring to the authority of a young woman's father in the formation of her romantic attachments, and I'm not referring to rigidly prescribed roles of parents and church in structuring the progress of a romantic relationship. Instead, by courtship I mean the unhurried development of a deep friendship between a man and a woman with the possibility of marriage, the enjoyment of time spent together without sexual involvement. Boundaries remain in place and serve to safeguard the relationship.

In today's dating scene many couples meet, begin dating and bypass courtship. They quickly begin to act like a married couple: grocery shopping, cooking dinner and eating together, sleeping overnight in the same bed, and sharing the bathroom. Some people want to test the relationship, wondering what it would be like to be married. Others fall into the pattern without much thought. They keep separate addresses, so they aren't officially living together, but they practice intermittent living together.

ANTICIPATION

When a relationship is in fast forward, people miss out on the wonderful stage of courtship. Forming a solid friendship through long conversations and shared experiences allows people to be known. Holding hands and taking long walks allows the relationship to unfold slowly. Grocery shopping and cooking dinner together may be an eventual part of courtship, but sleeping in the same bed and sharing a bathroom would not be. Words like *pursuing, longing* and *anticipation* are part of courtship, where people learn to savor every season of life.

Think of a little kid, Tommy, at Christmas. Tommy watches his parents decorate the house for Christmas. He helps to hang ornaments on the tree. Tommy digs through the piles of gifts under the Christmas tree and finds some with his name on them. He makes a tower by stacking his gifts, shaking some out of curiosity. The fancy wrapping paper and bows heightened his excitement. Special food is off limits until Christmas. His eyes dance, and his mouth salivates as he looks at the goodies.

On Christmas Eve, Tommy lies awake in his bed. He's too excited to sleep. Teaming with anticipation, he imagines what gifts he might get. He thinks of the candle he made his mom at school and can't wait to see her face when she opens it. He thinks of the fun he'll have when his favorite cousin comes over. He can hardly wait for Christmas, yet he must wait.

Morning finally comes, and Tommy races downstairs with his siblings. He opens his presents, dumps out the treasures in his stocking and feasts on special foods. His favorite cousin busts in the front door with the most prized Christmas gift tucked under an arm. Relatives fill the house, and the fireplace crackles. Life is good. Tommy's exhilarated!

Contrast this scenario with a different one. Tommy's mom comes in the back door from the garage, tossing a plastic bag from Target on his lap. "Here's your Christmas present." Without any fanfare, Tommy opens the bag and inside is a yearned-for toy. He's glad for the toy, but his experience wasn't much. He didn't have the opportunity to experience anticipation, longing or desire. The entire experience was diminished because they were lacking.

One of the delights of being human is experiencing anticipation. When a dating couple bypasses courtship and moves directly to acting married, they miss out on a wonderful stage of life.

They also set themselves up for hurt. When dating couples act like they're married, they bond. But to be known so deeply, to have shared life so completely only to break up leaves a person with self-doubt on a deep level. To be the rejected one can be devastating. After a simulated marriage, breaking up is similar to a divorce.

When people learn to love, to bond and to share deeply but then break up repeatedly, they learn to let go, to break bonds, to recover and to move on. This process is a setup for divorce in the future. For people who have experienced this pattern and eventually make it to the altar, it can be challenging to make the wedding and marriage special. One woman said to me, "We're trying to figure out how to make our wedding and marriage special. We've slept in the same bed more times than I can count, we've had sex, we've taken trips together and stayed in a hotel together, and the cake is for sure no big deal. We've decided that going to a new country on our honeymoon, one neither of us has ever been to, is the best way to introduce something new and special in our wedding and marriage."

The paradox is that our society treats sex as the most important thing in the world, something we can't possibly live without, and also as common and ordinary. With little thought, we give away our greatest treasures: our bodies, our hearts and our sexual passions. We feel robbed, but then we realize we have been the thieves.

5   Can we back up in our sexual relationship if we've gone too far?

Sarah came to our regular Monday afternoon appointment at the coffee shop, but I knew from her facial expression that this would not be a routine hour together. Her concerns spilled out. She and her boyfriend, Jason, had just come back from a weekend retreat with their Christian group. Both of them realized that a number of areas in their lives weren't pleasing to God. Top on this list was their sexual involvement.

Both of them were engineering students, and at the end of their stressful days, it was easier to just go back to his apartment, flop down on the bed and make out. One thing would lead to another. Even though they weren't having sexual intercourse, they both acknowledged that they needed to back up. Sarah even wondered if she should break up with Jason. As we talked, it became apparent that there were some wonderful aspects to their relationship and they both wanted to grow in their faith.

The scenario of Sarah and Jason is a common one. Sometimes breakups are appropriate, but let's consider when the relationship is basically good and healthy and both parties are seeking to follow God. Can a couple back up in their sexual involvement?

The answer is a resounding yes!

BACKWARD MEANS FORWARD

The first step is for both people to take time for personal reflection. They should spend time alone with God in prayer and ask him to show them boundaries for their sexual involvement and then share these boundaries with each other.

Talking with a trusted friend, like Sarah did with me, is another wise step. We need people in our lives who will allow us to open up about our struggles and mistakes and who will offer prayer and grace when we fail. Our quest for holiness is a corporate journey.

When a dating couple is too sexually involved, resentment often smolders beneath the surface. Each blames the other for their moral failings. Because of this, it's important for each member of the couple to have clear personal boundaries and to police themselves. One person can't be in charge of managing two sex drives.

It's also helpful to figure out your triggers. When do you tend to fall into sexual temptation? Think for a moment about the events that precede your sexual involvement or the conditions that set you up to fall. Sometimes choosing one thing also means saying yes to temptation. One student remarked to me, "We both know that when we decide to go down to the basement and lie on the couch to watch TV, things will get carried away." If you avoid the situations that tempt you, your battle will be easier. An alcoholic trying to stay sober doesn't go to a wine-tasting party.

What places or activities should you steer clear of? If being alone in your parents' home when they are out of town leads to sexual sin, then choose not to do that. If going back to a dorm room and locking the door causes you to overstep your boundaries, then consider that off limits. I know of some couples who have imposed curfews for themselves knowing that after 1:00 a.m. their judgment becomes impaired.

As I have checked with couples who have backed up on their sexual involvement, a number of unexpected benefits emerge. They look at one another with new and greater respect. They look at themselves as a couple and think, *I feel good about us!* We all know it's important to have a good self-image, but it's also important to have a good couple image. God intends that we be free from shame not only in our personal lives, but also in our dating relationships.

When couples back up on their sexual involvement, time and energy are redirected into something new. God often grows a new and beautiful aspect of their lives together. Sarah shared that because she and Jason were going to a coffee shop to talk instead of going back to his apartment, they had grown tremendously in their ability to communicate. She said, "We realized that as engineering students, we're not that good at talking and sharing our feelings. Our hours at the coffee shop have pushed us to share and communicate in ways that weren't automatic for us." Sarah and Jason are married now and have three kids. Those heart-to-heart talks at the campus coffee shop helped to establish a wonderful foundation of communication that serves them well as they build their lives together.

My husband, Bill, serves as a pastor. Several years ago, Rodney and Sharon, who were living together, began to attend our church. They asked my husband to officiate at their wedding. After he got to know them a little and found out they were both Christians, Bill said, "I want to help you build your relationship on Christ. I'm not in the business of performing ceremonies, but nurturing marriages." As they talked further, he went on to say, "In order to do that, you'll need to live separately and refrain from sex until after you're married." They were initially taken aback. They said it wasn't possible because of financial considerations, and they wouldn't be able to find a lease for six months.

That night Bill told me of his appointment with Rodney and Sharon. He said to me, "What if we offer to have one of them live with us rent free? If we're asking for this kind of commitment from them, we need to do whatever we can to help them toward holiness and a Christ-centered relationship." I agreed.

Within a few days, Rodney moved in and stayed with us for six months. Sharon and Rodney remained celibate. Rodney later commented that his own parents had divorced when he was young, so it was instructive to live with us and see the ups and downs of our marriage.

Rodney and Sharon chose to recommit themselves to chastity. With a season of sexual purity—a sexual fast—they gave God space to deepen their relationship with him. They realized that their sex life wasn't the only thing that God wanted to purify. Working with my husband, they learned what it meant to have a Christ-centered relationship.

When their wedding day came, it was a joyous celebration. How radically different their relationship was—founded on Christ.

Rodney and Sharon's marriage was a positive resolution to their situation. But never stay in a bad relationship because of sexual involvement. One young woman I counseled chose to stay in an unhealthy relationship. She was having sex with her boyfriend and felt like getting married was the only way to make it right. She explained her feelings to me: "I feel so horrible about giving my virginity away to him. The only way it can be made right is if I marry him." She tried for two years to get him to become a Christian, find a steady job and treat her with respect. None of those things happened. In time, she began to see that marrying him wasn't the solution to her sexual sin. God gave her the strength to break up with her boyfriend and turn to him for forgiveness and new life.

If you have already gone too far, don't despair. God is rich in forgiveness. God has the ability to purify you. He can make all things new. God's call on your life is to practice integrity, purity and chastity. Remember that your sexuality is a treasure—a gift given to you by God. Christ's death makes it possible for imperfect people like you and me to be washed clean, white as snow. This is exactly what God in his grace wants to do for you. He will change you from the inside out. Second Corinthians 5:17 says, "Therefore, if anyone is in Christ, the new creation has come: The old has gone, the new is here!"

Take a moment and pray. Tell God that you want to recommit to sexual purity. Tell him that you want him to be the Lord of your sex life. Ask him to make all things new in your life. These stories and countless others show that it's possible, with God's help, to back up sexually when you have gone too far.

6 What about oral sex?

When students are given an opportunity to write one of their questions about sex on an index card, the topic of oral sex always comes up.

People who teach high school sex ed classes and work in health clinics that serve college students have often encouraged single people to practice oral sex. Their reasoning goes like this: Young people can use oral sex as a safer option than sexual intercourse. Oral sex removes the concern of an unplanned pregnancy. Most singles consider oral sex far less intimate than vaginal sex. Furthermore, many people claim that oral sex doesn't count as sex. Bill Clinton's statement "I did not have sex with that woman" is well-known documentation of this thinking.

A *Washington Post* article, "Study: Half of All Teens Have Had Oral Sex," reports,

> Slightly more than half of American teenagers ages 15 to 19 have engaged in oral sex, with females and males reporting similar levels of experience, according to the most comprehensive national survey of sexual behaviors ever released by the federal government. The report released yesterday by the National Center for Health Statistics shows that the proportion increases with age to about 70 percent of all 18- and 19-year-olds.[6]

The prevalence of young single people engaging in oral sex is a major cultural shift. These statistics probably don't surprise you, but your parent's generation would be shocked.[7] The statistics for students who make abstinence pledges are comparable to the general teen population.

A survey by Northern Kentucky University revealed that 61 percent of students who made abstinence promises broke them. And of those who said they kept their pledges, 55 percent indicated they participated in oral sex. The survey queried 597 Northern Kentucky students, 16 percent of whom made pledges not to have sex until marriage. The study noted, however, that pledge-breakers delayed sex for a year longer than nonpledging teens—until an average of 17.6 years old. But pledge-makers who became pledge-breakers were less likely to use protection, such as condoms, when first having sex.[8]

How should a Christian think about oral sex? We need to go back to the fact that God is our Creator. He made us, and what he made is good. Psalm 139:13-14 says, "For you created my inmost being; you knit me together in my mother's womb. I praise you because I am fearfully and wonderfully made."

Your body is made by God, and all your body parts are good. The incarnation of Jesus is proof that the body isn't evil. God, who is completely and only good, had a body. You don't have any body parts that are bad or dirty. Some body parts are so precious that they are intended to be saved and shared with only one lucky person, your marriage partner.

When my kids were toddlers, I wanted to teach them this truth. When my son Luke was about three, he was running wildly up and down the hall after a bath. Little children are free spirits and love to run around naked after a bath. I called him back into the bathroom, combed his wet hair and said, "Luke, look at yourself in the mirror and say this Bible verse: 'I am fearfully and wonderfully made!'" Obediently, Luke hopped up on a stool, stood straight, looked into the mirror at his cute, naked body and said, in his three-year-old voice, "I am fearfully and wonderfully made!"

Next time you get out of the shower, look in the mirror and quote that verse. We often zero in on our imperfections, but the truth is that the human body is amazing and wonderful.

Given that we have no bad or dirty body parts, nothing is off limits for married couples in their sexual relationship. As long as sexual expression is done in love and with the consent of both partners, variety is fine. People should never be forced to participate in activities they consider undesirable, and nothing should be done that harms the body. Married couples have a lifetime to discover the delights of their sexual relationship. Over the years, things will evolve and change. New pleasures will be discovered. It's certainly possible to have a great sex life with or without oral sex.

Despite what you may have heard from your health teacher or friends, oral sex is an intimate act. It's far more intimate than a kiss. When it comes to dating, oral sex is off limits for good physical, spiritual and emotional reasons.

THE DAMAGE

How does oral sex damage a dating relationship? I recently met with Roshni, who told me she was having a hard time thinking of sex in marriage as something good. As we talked, it came out that she had engaged in oral sex with a boyfriend in high school. She said, "I thought this was something I had to do if I was in a dating relationship. It was nothing I wanted to do. It was an expectation, an obligation. I needed to do this to keep him." Her thoughts about sex in marriage had been warped: Sex is an obligation. Sex is for one person's pleasure. Sex is the price to pay to keep a relationship.

Even if oral sex is practiced for pleasure, it's still problematic for single people. Anytime we disconnect sexual pleasure from the loving, secure commitment of a lifelong marriage, we violate God's plan. Sexual activity of any kind is intended to bond us with our marriage partner.

Oral sex isn't safe sex either, because sexually transmitted diseases can be transmitted through oral sex. Oral sex has been associated in clinical studies with several infections, including gonorrhea, herpes, syphilis and the human papillomavirus, which has been linked to cervical cancer.[9]

If you have engaged in oral sex as a single person, don't think you're hopelessly flawed. Seek the forgiveness of God, who is rich in mercy. He can forgive you and wash you clean. Colossians 1:9-14 contains a prayer the apostle Paul wrote, which is my prayer for you. Drink in these rich words:

> For this reason, since the day we heard about you, we have not stopped praying for you. We continually ask God to fill you with the knowledge of his will through all the wisdom and understanding that the Spirit gives, so that you may live a life worthy of the Lord and please him in every way: bearing fruit in every good work, growing in the knowledge of God, being strengthened with all power according to his glorious might so that you may have great endurance and patience, and giving joyful thanks to the Father, who has qualified you to share in the inheritance of his people in the kingdom of light. For he has rescued us from the dominion of darkness and brought us into the kingdom of the Son he loves, in whom we have redemption, the forgiveness of sins.

Oral sex, like other forms of sex, should be saved for marriage.

7 How can we keep the boundaries we've set?

Ryan and Beth began dating at the end of their junior year of college. Both of them had been leaders in their Christian fellowship and were striving to follow God in their ministry endeavors and also in their relationships. One word that described both of them was *teachable*. They often asked for input, so when they asked me, "How can we keep the boundaries we have set and not fall into sexual sin?" I wasn't surprised.

I commended them for being proactive about holiness. So often, people wait until they've messed up before looking for answers. How wise is the couple who seeks to be pure from the start.

Both Ryan and Beth had spent time alone with God in prayer and come up with their personal boundaries. They had talked about these with one another, but how would they ever keep these standards? I shared the following ideas with them.

I recommended having accountability partners. We all need someone who will ask us tough questions about our personal lives. Find someone of the same sex who you can be totally honest with, someone who will give you grace when you fail but not let you get by with disobedience to the Lord.

Knowing that you'll be reporting to a trusted friend is often a huge deterrent. I was meeting regularly with one woman who said to me, "This weekend I'm traveling out of town to visit my boyfriend at his university. When you and I meet next week for our usual appointment, I want you to ask me exactly what happened between us. Ask me if we kept our standards of sexual purity." I told her I would ask her and that I would be praying for them to have a wonderful time together using nonsexual ways to convey their love.

The next week, I asked her about her time with her boyfriend. She told me that when she arrived, he wanted to show her his dorm room and introduce his roommate. When they got there, the roommate was gone. He shut the door and reached out to give her a huge embrace. After a long and meaningful hug, she said, "You need to know that I asked Mindy to hold me accountable for my sexual purity this weekend. I will be reporting everything that happens between us this weekend to Mindy."

The poor guy shrieked, took his hands off her and jumped backwards. He was a little freaked out by the thought, but afterward they laughed at his reaction. He respected her quest for holiness.

In addition to having an accountability partner, many people are helped by being part of a small group or community of grace where they can gather with fellow believers who are also seeking to live out biblical values of sexual purity. People often think chastity is the responsibility of the dating couple alone and fail to see the help that a faith community can offer.

Another idea is for a young couple to seek out an older couple who can offer help, not only on sexual temptation but also on communication, conflict resolution and the like.

In addition to having an accountability partner, small group and mentors, it's good to think through how to structure time together to avoid being bombarded by temptation. Going to public places that offer some privacy—a coffee shop, a quiet restaurant or a park where children play—can provide a place to have heart-to-heart talks without a sexually charged atmosphere. How carried away can you get when the perky server reappears every twelve minutes asking to refill your coffee cup?

When our family lived in Ann Arbor, we used to love to take the kids to a park where the Huron River flowed. In spring, the river raged with speed and strength after collecting the winter's melted snow. Our kids were fascinated by the river and would throw sticks and leaves in to see the water pull it quickly downstream. I would warn them not to get too close so they wouldn't fall in and be swept away. "If you don't want to fall into the river, then don't play on the slippery riverbank. Stay three feet away from the river's edge, and you'll never fall in."

This is a picture of how we should act in our quest for purity. "If you don't want to fall into the river, then don't play on the slippery riverbank," is a good mantra for us in all areas of holiness. In the same way that a shopaholic should not spend leisure time in the mall, so those seeking sexual purity should avoid any place that provides opportunity for them to fall into sin.

LOVE LANGUAGES

One of the challenges for couples who want to remain sexually pure is how to convey love in nonsexual ways. In his book *The Five Love Languages* Gary Chapman[10] describes five ways to convey love:

- Words of affirmation
- Quality time spent together
- Gifts
- Acts of service
- Physical touch

After reading the book, I personally think there's a sixth love language: food! Cooking a special meal for the person you're dating or showing up with a well-loved snack at the library for a study break are wonderful ways to say I love you.

Developing these other love languages not only maintains the purity of the dating relationship but also grows some wonderful new aspects. In a healthy marriage, couples demonstrate radical love to one another in a variety of ways—apart from sex.

Learning the love language of the person you're dating is important. What conveys love to you may not convey love to the person you're dating. Talk together. Look over the list and dialogue about what makes each of you feel loved. Having other ways to convey love helps diminish the need to express love physically, which helps you keep the sexual boundaries you've set but still allows for continuing growth in your relationship.

8   What's so bad about porn?

As I sat in the coffee shop with Thomas, conversation came easily. He was a former football player, highly social and loved to talk on a wide variety of subjects. Our lives had crossed paths in a campus fellowship and church, so we sat drinking coffee and getting caught up. Our conversation turned to his hope of one day being married and raising a family. As a devoted Christian, he was careful in his interpersonal relationships with women.

Thomas said something that caught me off-guard. He shared that he was using pornography as a way to avoid sexual involvement with women he knew. He said, "I don't want to mess up some girl's life. At least with pornography, I'm not messing up anyone's life." Thomas planned to stop using porn when he got married.

To him, using pornography was less harmful than real sex and was a back door route to holiness. While it's true that a person can avoid sexually transmitted diseases and avoid unplanned pregnancies by using pornography, it's far from harmless. Thomas is one of many single men who think marriage and a legitimate sex partner will be the end of his desire for pornography. Probably it won't. Many married men who dearly love their wives struggle with pornography.

My husband and I were meeting with a young couple, Ricardo and Cyndi, whose marriage was nearly shipwrecked due to Ricardo's ongoing use of pornography. Prior to their marriage, Ricardo had shared his attachment to pornography with Cyndi. They both were leaders in their campus fellowship and were optimistic that marriage would take away Ricardo's attraction to pornography. They reasoned that if he had a real sex partner and was fulfilled with her, his habit of using pornography would disappear.

As the four of us sat in my husband's office, I pensively stared at Ricardo's exceptionally beautiful wife. I was totally at a loss. I finally said to the husband, "I'm sorry to be stupid, but I just don't get it. You have this unbelievably beautiful wife, and yet you choose pornography? How could anything electronic be better than this amazing, beautiful, real-life woman?"

His answer was direct and honest. "You see, she's complicated. Sometimes she has a bad day at work and isn't in the mood for sex. Sometimes she has her period and is unavailable. When we do come together, I have to think about what she likes and wants, how to please her. She's complicated. But when I turn to pornography, it's all about me. Any time, any day, I can instantly find satisfaction. In my sexual fantasy world, I'm super attractive. Women want me; women are always available to me and place no demands on me." His incredible honesty gave me a window into his struggle. I realized in that moment how his single years using pornography had shaped him sexually.

THE CURE FOR SELFISHNESS

God intends sex to draw us out of our selfish *me* world and help us connect with another person. As we become one flesh with another person, we take on their concerns, passions, problems, dreams and ambitions. *Me* becomes *we.* Probably the greatest danger in using pornography is that it short-circuits the unity of a sexual experience and makes it a totally selfish act.

Pornography makes real people and real relationships disappointing by developing the expectations that they will be as beautiful or handsome as the airbrushed movie stars and require no sacrifice. Relationships with real people are often complicated, messy and draining. We have to lay aside our own agendas to seek the good of another human being.

Another problem with using pornography is that it develops an appetite for a dark form of sexuality. Men derive a false sense of power from watching women be humiliated and degraded. God's beautiful gift is twisted through violence, degrading acts and sexual abuse of children. This sets up users for an unhealthy duality in sex: pure and loving sex between a husband and wife contrasted with dark, dirty sexual fantasies that will never be fulfilled in marriage.

An increasing number of women also use pornography. An article in *Today's Christian Woman* reported that "one out of every six women, including Christians, struggles with an addiction to pornography."[11] One woman interviewed said, "I thought this would be an answer to my loneliness, but it only made it worse. I was so ashamed of what I was doing I isolated myself."

Many people use pornography to medicate unwanted feelings. Pornography can alter a person's mood by creating excitement for people who are bored, relaxation for people who are stressed, and the illusion of intimacy for people who are lonely.

WHAT LIES BENEATH THE SURFACE

If you're using pornography, look beneath the surface and ask, "What negative emotion am I trying to medicate with pornography?" God desires to enter into those painful places in our souls and bring his companionship and his healing power.

When we use pornography, we often justify it with a sense of entitlement.

- I've worked so hard today, I deserve this little treat.

- My partner doesn't have as big of a need for sex as I do. This helps us balance out.

- I've tried to find a real relationship but nothing works out. I deserve to have my sexual needs met.

Telling ourselves these things makes using pornography seem legitimate. What big or little lies do you tell yourself to justify acting out with pornography?

Take stock of your fantasies. When you have sexual fantasies, is there a recurring theme? What's going on? Who shows up? What's the scene of your sexual fantasies? Sexual fantasies are a way to heal the wounded places in the soul. They bring missing pieces like love and affirmation. Ricardo told us that he had recurring fantasies about attractive women wanting him, seeking him out and finding him irresistible. He said in high school that he wasn't popular and had trouble getting a date for the dance. The popular girls ignored him. He longed so deeply to be chosen, to be wanted. All that was corrected in his sexual fantasies.

Some people believe that an addiction to pornography is the hardest addiction to break. There must be a radical renunciation of the fantasy world that porn users construct within. It takes courage to live in real life with a real person, but the rewards are worth it. Ricardo confessed that part of him wanted to give up his addiction to pornography but part of him didn't. He was conflicted. Ricardo was hoping for magical deliverance from his addiction, but the truth is his healing started when he was willing to completely renounce his addiction to pornography and face the truth that he was using pornography to self-medicate his unwanted emotions. It was hard work. Ricardo also began pursuing better ways of self-care—working out, eating healthy food, and getting adequate sleep. He realized he didn't have deep, meaningful relationships with men. It was hard for him to think of even one guy he could call a good friend, so he set a goal to develop a network of men he could be authentic with and enjoy socializing with.

The single best way to break free from pornography is to pursue meaningful friendships with men *and* women. Often loneliness and isolation cause people to turn to pornography. Being meaningfully involved in a Christian community, serving alongside like-minded people and entering into the joys and sorrows of life with other people makes us alive on the inside. Joining a recovery group or finding an accountability partner is crucial. We all need people who will walk with us on the path of discipleship. Becoming holy is a corporate journey.[12]

Pornography is ultimately unfulfilling and a poor substitute for delight and joy in God's good creation. Cultivating positive habits like joining a sports team or a Bible study can help us redirect our sexual energies in more constructive ways. Think of replacing the pleasure of pornography with a higher pleasure.

9 Is masturbation wrong?

This is one of the most frequently asked questions about sexuality on college campuses. It's reported that 95 percent of men masturbate (some think the other 5 percent are lying!) and about 40 percent of women masturbate, so it's a topic of concern to most people.

One of the truly difficult things in our society is the gap between the early age of sexual awakening and the later age of marriage. We live in a sexually charged society where watching a harmless TV program assaults us with sexual content through advertisements for toothpaste, cars and tropical vacations. Magazine covers at the grocery store and billboards flash images that intensify our sexual longings.

Although the Bible is frank and graphic on the topic of sex, it never mentions masturbation, not in the Old Testament, not in the New Testament, not in Jesus' teaching. The silence of Scripture should make us think that excessive concern in this area may be ill-founded.

THE PROBLEM OF ONAN

One passage used by some religious leaders to teach on masturbation is the story of Onan in Genesis 38. This historical narrative starts when Er, Onan's older brother, dies before having any children. His widow, Tamar, is left childless. The Jewish people practiced levirate marriage, through which a legal obligation was placed on the nearest male relative to sleep with the widow to produce an heir for the deceased brother. Judah, the father of Er and Onan, exhorts Onan to make good on this obligation:

> Then Judah said to Onan, "Sleep with your brother's wife and fulfill your duty to her as a brother-in-law to raise up offspring

for your brother." But Onan knew that the child would not be his; so whenever he slept with his brother's wife, he spilled his semen on the ground to keep from providing offspring for his brother. What he did was wicked in the LORD's sight; so he put him to death also. (Genesis 38:8-10)

It has always been hard for me to understand why Christian teachers have used this text to teach on masturbation, since Onan is having sex with a woman, not masturbating. There are two evils here: Onan wasn't fulfilling his obligation under the rules of Israel (see Deuteronomy 25:5-6), and Onan was exploiting the social custom and his sister-in-law for his selfish sexual pleasure. This biblical text could spawn some interesting dialogues about sex and family responsibility, but it doesn't help us with the question of masturbation.

It's not wrong to touch one's own sexual body parts. We do this every day in the shower. The evil comes when we fantasize about having sex with someone who isn't our marriage partner; it's almost impossible to masturbate without lusting.

Jesus said in Matthew 5:27-28, "You have heard that it was said, 'You shall not commit adultery.' But I tell you that anyone who looks at a woman lustfully has already committed adultery with her in his heart." In this command, Jesus raised the bar. Not only is adultery wrong, but even lust is wrong.

Solo sex wrenches sex out of the context of relationship. Through masturbation people seek the gratification of sex without being in a real relationship with a real person.

C. S. Lewis wrote about masturbation in a personal letter to a friend. His words are insightful:

For me the real evil of masturbation would be that it takes an appetite which leads the individual out of himself to complete and correct his own personality in that of another and turns it back; sends the man back into the prison of himself, there to keep a harem of imaginary brides. And this harem, once admitted, works against his ever getting out and really uniting with a real woman. For the harem is always accessible, always subservient, calls for no sacrifices or adjustments, and can be endowed with erotic and psychological attractions which no real woman can rival. Among those shadowy brides he is always adored, always the perfect lover; no demand is ever made on his unselfishness, nor mortification ever imposed on his vanity. In the end, they become merely the medium through which he increasingly adores himself.[13]

Our sexual desires are intended to pull us out of ourselves and to seek completion in another. When we long for completion in another and cannot have that satisfaction, masturbation relieves sexual tension but leaves us ultimately unfulfilled. Masturbation often reflects a loneliness and longing for love, yet the shame and secrecy of the habit sometimes drive a person further away from others.

One of the dangers of masturbation is that it can cause people to think of their sexual longings and desires as bad. Lisa McMinn states,

Many of us are neo-Gnostic without realizing it, holding on to a dualistic idea about the body and soul, believing we can separate the two. We rank the body as less valuable than the soul, as something useful and good but also base, crude, in need of chastisement and discipline so that the desires of the body do not lead the soul astray. . . . An incarnational perspective does not accept this separation of body and soul. Indeed, our soul's longing for connection and intimacy is expressed in the body's desire for sexual fulfillment. . . .

When masturbation is understood as a reflection of one's aloneness and loneliness, it takes on significance for the soul. Our redemption is for our bodies as well as our soul, not because they are two separate entities but because they are one. The redemptive challenge becomes finding healthy ways to engage the self with others so that the need to satisfy longing by engaging with one's self in masturbation is minimized.[14]

REDIRECTING SEXUAL DESIRES

Masturbation is an attempt to fulfill our desire for intimacy. Developing deeper relationships and becoming more meaningfully involved in the community of Christians seems to diminish the desire to masturbate. Even when it's not possible to have sexual intimacy, it's possible to have emotional intimacy with other people and spiritual intimacy with God. Our sexual desires are good and God-given, but it is important to find ways to redirect sexual desire when we are not married.

Stan, a college student, found that his struggle with masturbation diminished with two decisions he made. He joined a weekly accountability group with other men also struggling with masturbation. Knowing he wasn't alone and having open conversations about sex with trusted friends brought an honesty and intimacy he had never experienced. Their brotherhood was meaningful.

Stan also decided to spend his spring break building a home on a Habitat for Humanity trip with his campus friends. Hanging out for the week, cooking meals, traveling and working side by side in grubbies set the stage for making deep friendships with a group of men and women. Swinging a hammer and hoisting dry wall gave him a chance to express his masculinity in positive ways. As he got to know the Habitat family who would move into the house, he developed a concern for the poor. Getting outside of himself and helping someone less fortunate in the company of friends was deeply satisfying. These friendships continued back on campus. As his isolation and loneliness diminished, so did his need to masturbate.

Some Christians condemn masturbation because it is usually linked with lust. Other Christians leave the door open, seeing it as less harmful than intercourse and other sexual activities between two unmarried people. In my opinion, concern over masturbation seems warranted when masturbation is compulsive and addictive or when masturbation prevents people from having real and authentic relationships.

Masturbation grows out of our desire for love and intimacy, a longing that is good and God-given, yet masturbation is an impoverished substitute. It reminds us that we live in a fallen world as imperfect people. Only in heaven will our deepest longings be fulfilled.

10 I'm addicted to male attention. How can I break free?

Kristen carelessly tossed her backpack on the floor and slumped into the chair. She had always been a straight shooter in our appointments together, yet her opening comment to me was even more passionate than usual.

"I've realized that I'm addicted to male attention!" Sipping her latte she continued, "Two days ago, I woke up and put on some cute shorts and a tank top, did my hair and my makeup, and left for class. As I walked across the quad, I noticed that guys' heads turned to look at me. Several guys gave me that look that said, 'Wow, she's hot!' and

I felt wonderful! All day long I was happy as I fed off the attention of being noticed and admired. I felt great about me, and I felt great about life.

"But yesterday, my alarm didn't go off, so I overslept. When I realized what time it was, I rushed out of bed, picked up some grungy sweats on the floor, threw my hair in a ponytail and dashed off to class. I didn't care what I looked like or that I didn't have makeup on. All I cared about was making it to my organic chemistry class. As I walked across campus the same way I walked the day before, I suddenly realized that no guys were turning to look at me. No guys were giving me the she's-hot look. I had somehow become invisible. I felt like crap.

"That whole day was a nightmare. I kept feeling worse and worse. All day long I was in despair about not being noticed and admired, but then I began to be in utter despair when I realized I'm addicted to male attention. How sick is that?"

I leaned forward and said to Kristen, "Let me just tell you as a middle-aged woman the male attention thing doesn't last. Some day you'll be married to one man who will fall asleep in front of a Cubs game. Hot guys you meet around town start making comments about how you remind them of their mom. You have to find something more enduring to build your identity on."

Kristen found that her happiness was like the Dow Jones stock index. It would rise and fall on a daily basis. Receiving male attention made it a good day; being ignored made it a bad day. Kristen isn't unusual. Magazines, TV commercials and the media feed us the line that a woman's worth is bound up in her appearance.

It was easy for me to connect with Kristen because I've struggled with the same problem. I grew up with three sisters and no brothers. All the significant relationships in my life were female—except for my father. My dad was an energetic, fun-loving and generous man. He loved us and worked hard to provide for us. As a little girl I wanted desperately to have his love and approval, but his frequent travel for work and critical words often left me feeling wounded. His daily martinis sometimes made things worse.

When I was six years old, I came down with polio. Lying in my hospital bed, I would watch the doorway hoping my dad would come visit me. He never came once to see me. Years later, I know he did care about me. He just couldn't muster up the internal strength to walk into a polio ward and see all the sick children, some crippled and some in iron lungs. But as a little girl I felt so abandoned by him.

During my adolescent years, this father-hunger and lack of men in my life left me starving for male attention. I wanted desperately to be noticed, admired and loved. I was just like Kristen. I fed off male attention. I dressed to elicit attention.

I became a Christian during my sophomore year of college while living in a sorority house on the campus of the University of Illinois. A few months after my conversion, I was getting ready to go out to the bars with my sorority sisters. As I got dressed in bar clothes, a little voice from within said, "Why are you dressing like that? Why do you try to make men's heads turn? Do you really want men—other people's boyfriends and husbands—to lust after you?" God was beginning to dismantle the false sense of worth I gained from male attention. I changed outfits. Eventually I got rid of certain clothes. I began to see that my heavenly father's love for me could fill the father-hunger in my heart.

The Sunday after I met with Kristen, I worked in the two- and three-year-old room at our church nursery and was astonished at the innocent comments made to our young kids. "Anna don't you look pretty today! I love your blue-checked dress and pretty socks!" Even

a two-year-old girl in the church nursery was being valued for her
appearance!

IDENTITY IN CHRIST

Christian women have something much more enduring to build their
identity on. God is our creator. We belong to him and are his precious
daughters. He chose the color of our eyes, the shape of our nose and
everything else about our appearance. He also chose our ethnic background. We are his workmanship.

The human body is beautiful. The Bible affirms the goodness of
the human body in Psalm 139:13-14: "For you created my inmost
being; you knit me together in my mother's womb. I praise you because I am fearfully and wonderfully made." In *Wanting to Be Her:
Body Image Secrets Victoria Won't Tell You,* Michelle Graham says,

> Think about a continuum between two extremes: body obses-
> sion and body neglect. A balanced approach avoids both ends.
> . . . Body obsessions are rooted in the heart, travel to the mind
> and bear fruit in our actions. . . . Does this behavior express
> worry about my appearance? Is it based on fear of what others
> think of me? Does it drive me to focus too much on impressing
> others instead of resting in God's love for me? Has it been occu-
> pying an inordinate amount of my time? My money? My
> thoughts? My conversation? . . . On the other hand, body ne-
> glect would manifest in any behaviors that hurt my body or in
> any failure to take care of it. Often such neglect results from
> shame, control, laziness or an overly busy lifestyle. It can even
> reflect a misguided idea that taking care of our bodies is not
> spiritual, that those who love Jesus are not concerned with their
> physical selves.[15]

All people display something of God's beauty. We do well to know what colors look good on us and what clothing enhances our appearance. Christians shouldn't fall off the fence in either being obsessed about appearance (thinking it's the most important thing about them and the basis for affirmation) or neglecting their personal appearance (thinking it's a sign of godliness).

We tend to think of our bodies as belonging to us, but our bodies really belong to God. First Corinthians 6:19-20 says, "Do you not know that your bodies are temples of the Holy Spirit, who is in you, whom you have received from God? You are not your own; you were bought at a price. Therefore honor God with your bodies." What a radical orientation to think that the body belongs to God.

I grew up in Northbrook, Illinois, a wealthy suburb in the Chicago area. My dad was a businessman, and my mother was a professional dancer before getting married. My parents both placed great value on appearance, as did their circle of friends and business associates. In fact, how a person looked was of utmost importance.

Part of my journey with Christ has been the process of dismantling the false belief that my worth is tied to my appearance. I have struggled to reject the lie that I must look a certain way to be lovable. I have embraced the truth that God loves me just the way I am. I'm trying to hang on to the truth that I'm not losing my value or beauty in God's eyes as I grow older. Every person is a beautiful creation of God. Ultimately our worth comes from God. As women we are daughters of the King of kings. I think many women will someday arrive in heaven, behold Jesus and say, "I never knew how beautiful I was. I measured my appearance against an arbitrary standard. If only I had seen myself with your eyes, Jesus."

God wants to use our hands to touch the world with his love, God wants to use our feet to take the good news of the gospel to unreached people and God wants to use our mouths to speak words of instruction and healing. Our bodies belong to him.

But in addition to our physical bodies, God created within us a soul to know him and connect with him in a love relationship, a sacred romance. Our capacity to know and connect with God is perhaps the best thing about us. The Bible tells us that God, Jesus and the Holy Spirit will come and take up residence within our hearts (John 14:23). It's God living within us, flooding our hearts with his love, that gives us a deep and rock-solid sense of well being.

God has also given us gifts and talents and abilities to use in his vast world. He wants us to partner with him in his mission around the world. He wants to use our lives as a conduit to dispense his amazing love to other people. Seeing ourselves as women who can garner male attention is far too small. We are created for much greater things!

11 How can I see women as more than sex objects?

Nathan grew up in a household of four brothers where life was a revolving door of baseball games, soccer practices and neighborhood pickup basketball games. He and his brothers shared everything: sporting equipment, Nintendo, CDs and a beat-up red Honda with 180,000 miles. They also shared a few *Playboy* magazines. Void of sisters and with family life high on sports and testosterone, it was hard for Nathan to think of women apart from their sexuality. Nathan began experimenting with sex at an early age.

Nathan came to the university as a self-proclaimed atheist, but he was invited by his roommate to a Bible study. After several months of questioning, Nathan gave his heart to Christ and began his journey of faith. At a Christian retreat after a Q & A session on sexuality, Nathan posed this question: "How can I see women as more than sex objects?"

For starters, Nathan needed to realize that he's living in a sex-charged society. Philip Yancey in his booklet, *Designer Sex,* comments on how things have changed since the time of Martin Luther in the sixteenth century. "In Luther's day, a teenage boy might get a glimpse of a girl's bare legs as she stomped on grapes or bent over to draw water from a well. He did not face the temptations of MTV reports on co-eds who flash their breasts on the beach during spring break; he did not have photos of Britney and J. Lo and Anna Kournikova streaming digitally over his DSL line into the privacy of his bedroom."[16]

Sexualized dress of women isn't just among twentysomethings. Even grandmothers, aunts and middle-aged bank tellers wear provocative clothing. Perhaps the biggest shock is the grade school girls dressed like hookers, carrying their American Girl dolls. Even children's clothes have a sleaze factor.

The movie *Legally Blonde* may be a chick flick, but it contains a real lesson for men. Elle Woods, played by Reese Witherspoon, is a beautiful blonde sorority girl who people value for her good looks. Elle's world collapses when she's dumped by Warner Huntington III who goes off to Harvard Law School. Elle follows him and also enrolls in Harvard Law School. What starts out as a ploy to get her boyfriend back ends up as a fight for justice, respect and honor.

Emmett Richmond, played by Luke Wilson, ends up being the real hero of the movie. He sees Elle as a whole person. He mentors her through tough professors and supports her when she takes on a difficult case in the courtroom. Emmett respects Elle and believes in her.

Elle has never encountered any man who treats her the way Emmett does.

The first time I saw *Legally Blonde,* I was with my daughter Meredith. When we left the theater and got in the car I started crying. My daughter asked, "Why are you crying? Mom, that was a comedy!"

I said, "I'm crying because I see my story in her story. I'm not as pretty as Elle Woods, and I'm not as smart, but for much of my life I felt like my value was in my appearance. Your dad was the Emmett Richmond in my life. When we began dating he was interested in my thoughts. He wanted to know my spiritual gifts. He wanted to sacrifice for me to become all I could be in Christ. He suggested I go to seminary. He suggested I go on InterVarsity staff. He saw what I could become and believed in me."

Men who don't want to treat women like sex objects need to be Emmett Richmond to the women they encounter. When men see the potential in women and support their development and take their thoughts seriously, they create an environment where their gifts are unleashed. Then they transcend the shallowness of seeing women as sex objects and see them as whole persons.

JESUS AND THE SAMARITAN WOMAN

Emmett's interaction with Elle reminds me of Jesus' interaction with the woman at the well in John 4. The woman Jesus spoke to was, frankly, the hometown slut. She had had five husbands and was living with guy number six. She was the kind of woman you don't want your husband talking to at the neighborhood party!

Jesus overcame three cultural barriers when he talked with her:

- Jews didn't associate with Samaritans.
- Jewish men didn't talk to women other than their wives.

• Rabbis didn't talk to women of questionable morality.

Other men had seen this woman's sexual potential, but Jesus saw her spiritual potential. Jesus engaged her in a lofty theological discussion. He saw her as possessing a mind that could grasp deep spiritual truths. She was the first person to whom he disclosed his identity as Messiah. He looked beneath the surface of her life and saw that hopping from man to man was her quest for love. He knew the deepest needs of her soul and offered her living water to provide true satisfaction.

As the story unfolds, this woman became the PR agent for Jesus. She's the one he chose to herald the good news of his coming. (I love that part of the story!) Jesus chose the town outcast to be his PR agent. At the beginning of the story she came alone at noon to draw water (done to avoid people), but by the end of the story she was the center of the town buzz. She was somebody. Jesus gave her a new identity. I'm sure the woman thought, "Wow, no one has ever treated me like Jesus did!" Jesus saw what she could become. To be like Christ is to look at women and see their longings and their potential, not just a collection of beautiful body parts. Nathan, and all men, find in Jesus the role model of a man who treats women with respect.

THE LORD LOOKS AT THE HEART

First Samuel 16 describes the scene of a religious ceremony. Everyone in attendance was dressed up, and the prophet Samuel was ready to begin the proceedings. The parade of potential candidates for king began. The oldest son, Eliab, a good-looking, tall guy was first. If he were alive today, he might be on the cover of *GQ* magazine. Samuel thought to himself, *Wow, here's the man! He's the one God wants for sure!* Even the most devout person in Israel, Samuel, was ready to anoint the one who looked good on the outside.

But God spoke into Samuel's ear one of the most remarkable comments in all of Scripture. It speaks volumes about who God is and what God values. "But the LORD said to Samuel, 'Do not consider his appearance or his height, for I have rejected him. The LORD does not look at the things human beings look at. People look at the outward appearance, but the LORD looks at the heart" (1 Samuel 16:7).

God is so different from people. We're enamored with the beautiful people of this world. Think about Facebook, MySpace and all the drama of getting your perfect photo posted. We live in a beauty-driven society. But as Christ is formed in us, we'll change the way we view people. The inner life takes on more meaning. Proverbs 31:30 says, "Charm is deceptive, and beauty is fleeting; but a woman who fears the LORD is to be praised."

Movies, magazines and TV portray women in sexually charged ways, but some are worse than others. Nathan may want to avoid the ones that run against his efforts to see women as whole people. I also recommended that Nathan seek friendships with women he's not physically attracted to, who don't present him with sexual tension. To spend time with a woman and learn of her hopes, dreams, fears, likes and beliefs is to make her go from one-dimensional—a body—to multidimensional—a whole person. By doing this, Nathan will learn to embrace the wonderful complexity of women. Spending time with groups of people who hang out together and relate as brothers and sisters in Christ will help him see women as fellow human beings.

The apostle Paul wrote to the young man Timothy, his ministry partner, "Do not rebuke an older man harshly, but exhort him as if he were your father. Treat younger men as brothers, older women as mothers, and younger women as sisters, with absolute purity" (1 Timothy 5:1-2). If Nathan can see young women as sisters and older women as mothers as Paul directed Timothy, it puts women in an entirely different category.

Women can help men like Nathan. They can refrain from creating a sexually charged atmosphere by considering the way they dress and the way they act. I find it ironic that a man can be charged with sexual harassment for saying, "You have nice legs" to a woman, but a woman isn't held accountable for showing up at the office in a see-through, low-cut blouse and a short skirt. In the name of freedom, she can dress as she pleases.

I don't intend to communicate that men's sexual purity is the responsibility of women. That view presupposes that temptation is located in women's bodies and that men's sexual lusts and appetites are beyond their control. But women should be mindful of the great number of men—married and single—who struggle with lust. The way women dress shapes the way they will be treated and thought of.

The apostle Paul writes in Romans 12:2, "Do not conform to the pattern of this world, but be transformed by the renewing of your mind." Coming to Christ means having your mind transformed, having a whole new way to look at life, money, the poor, power and even women. Part of Nathan's journey with Christ will be having God reprogram his mind to see women holistically, body, soul and spirit.

12 Will my struggle with sexual temptation end when I'm married?

To put it bluntly, no, your struggle with sexual temptation won't end when you get married. This is one of many myths about marriage.

Many single people feel that if they can just stand up against sexual temptation until their wedding day, they'll be finished with sexual temptation once and for all. But if all temptation ended at marriage, there would be no affairs, no married people visiting pornographic websites, no office flirtations, and no lustful thoughts. Being in a loving and deeply connected marriage with a good sex life greatly diminishes sexual temptation, but it's naïve to think that all sexual temptations will stop.

Some people report an increase in sexual temptation. For people who have been chaste before marriage, the sexual activity of marriage gives them a knowledge—and temptation—they never had before.

Books and sermons often assume sexual temptation is present for married men, but not for married women. Mary Ellen Ashcroft writes of women's struggles in *Temptations Women Face:*

"Why have I been given the impression ever since I became a Christian that sex and lust are not a problem for women?" says Emily, the wife of a minister. "I regularly struggle with strong sexual feelings for men other than my husband. I fantasize about them.

"I also avoid them," Emily continued, "When I have a crush on someone, I just don't go anywhere that he might be. I wouldn't dream of getting myself into a compromising situation with a man. But talks and books and sermons and talk shows make it sound as if Christian women, or maybe particularly wives, don't struggle with this. When the Bible talks about our 'unruly passions' that need to be controlled, I know just what it means."[17]

When two people are married, they get to know one another; the good, the bad and the ugly. Bad hair days, bad breath and bad moods are all part of marriage. Unlike dating, when time together is planned and limited, married people are together 24/7. Petty squabbles can occur in the course of simply living life in the same space. Sharing space and being together for days at a time inevitably force our dark side (those traits and habits that we try to hide) to come out.

Being married and seeing our spouses at their worst sets us up for unrealistic comparisons. Officemates only see us showered and dressed for work and on our best behavior. Conversely, we see them only at their best. We don't see them on Saturday in their grungies when they're in a bad mood. It's so easy to be sucked into flattery that might come from people we have limited contact with.

CULTIVATING FIDELITY

What can single people do before marriage that cultivates fidelity if they do marry? Chastity in singleness is the exact same spiritual discipline as fidelity in marriage. Cultivating purity and integrity as a single person leads to fidelity in marriage.

The Song of Songs, dedicated to romantic love in marriage, concludes:

> Place me like a seal over your heart, like a seal on your arm; for love is as strong as death, its jealousy unyielding as the grave. It burns like blazing fire, like a mighty flame. Many waters cannot quench love; rivers cannot sweep it away. If one were to give all the wealth of one's house for love, it would be utterly scorned. (Song of Songs 8:6-7)

What can we learn from this rich biblical text?

"Place me like a seal over your heart" is a statement of belonging. In ancient times, the seal was a mark of ownership, saying to the world, "This belongs to me." When we get married we not only belong to God, but we also belong to the person we marry. A wedding ring is a public statement of belonging. Being married means saying to the world we're no longer available; we're taken.

"Love is as strong as death; its jealousy unyielding as the grave" teaches us that as the grave won't give up the dead, so the lover won't give up his beloved. Married love is tenacious and won't quit when the going gets tough.

"It burns like blazing fire" speaks of the enduring nature of love. It's God and his love that continue to kindle the flame of love. The God who brings you together will keep you together. Love that lasts a lifetime needs the resource of God's love.

"Many waters cannot quench love; rivers cannot sweep it away." This is a word picture of the awesome power of love to withstand adversity. There is staying power in love that is built on God.

"If one were to give all the wealth of one's house for love, it would be utterly scorned." Last of all, we see that true love can't be purchased. Any attempt to buy love is despised and rejected.

These analogies bind together to teach us that marital love is the strongest, most enduring force in the realm of human experience.

A number of years ago, after talking with several married people who were struggling with sexual attraction to someone other than their mates, I cried out to God, "Lord, why don't you just cauterize our sex drive when we get married? Why don't you flip some switch in heaven and make married people have sexual feelings only toward the one person they're married to? This whole sexual part of us is too complicated."

God did not give me an answer that day, but as I have pondered this further, I've realized that true love involves choice. Being married means choosing to turn away from other attractive options and channeling all your passion into one special person: your marriage partner. Every day since I married, I have said yes to loving Bill Meier. I have said, "I choose you!"

If you marry, sexual temptations won't vanish. You'll probably be attracted to other people, but with God's help and some hard but honest talks with your mate, you can remain faithful. Staying faithful to God and staying faithful to your marriage partner go hand in hand. Just remember to look at the one you married each day and say in your heart, "I choose you."

13 If I have been sexually abused, can I still have a good sex life in marriage?

Keisha and I sat in the basement of the union drinking our smoothies while upbeat music played in the background, but the festive atmosphere was in sharp contrast to Keisha's story. As she poured out the tale of her parents' divorce and the molestation by her stepfather, my heart broke. For many years, Keisha had hated men, but her newfound faith in Jesus was causing her to rethink her views of men, sex, relationships, her abuse and just about everything.

About one in three women and one in five men report having been sexually molested to some extent.[18] The abuser can be a stepfather, an uncle, a cousin, a sister, a youth pastor, a priest, a school teacher, a family friend. Anyone. Seventy-five to 95 percent of the time, the victim knows the abuser.

Many people report that after being abused they feel dirty, spoiled and shameful. Many kids think they must have done something bad to deserve it, when this is never the case. Often victims go to great lengths to keep the abuse a secret for fear of upsetting the family. One young man told me, "If my dad found out that my uncle abused me, he'd kill him, and I don't want my dad going to jail."

Even when people open up, often their stories aren't believed. Keisha told her mother about her sexual abuse, and her mother's response was, "Your stepfather would never do anything like that. Don't ever mention this again, or you'll upset the family." Perhaps it was too painful for Keisha's mother to admit that her husband was unfaithful to her, especially with her own daughter.

People who have been sexually abused respond in a variety of ways: Some develop a huge fear of sex; some become promiscuous figuring they're already spoiled and dirty so there isn't anything to save for marriage. Some people develop depression, eating disorders or problems sleeping. Even excessive busyness can be a strategy to mask the sadness inside. For Keisha it was a combination of hating men and being promiscuous.

Denial and repression are often used to keep the bad memories underground until a time when the abuse victim feels safe enough and strong enough to open up the painful storehouse of memories and admit that something terribly wrong happened.

HARD WORK AND WILLINGNESS

The wonderful news is that Jesus Christ can heal the wounds left by sexual abuse. It *is* possible to recover from sexual abuse and have a good sex life in marriage. But to do so requires hard work and willingness to walk into your pain. It also means tapping into the healing power of Jesus. If possible, it's best to begin the journey of healing before you're married.

Begin by finding a trusted friend or counselor to open up to, since wounds fester in the dark. Bringing the truth into the light of Christ dispels its power in our lives. Find a Christian counselor who has experience working with sexual abuse survivors. Become involved in a Christian community of people who know your story, believe your story and love you. Ask trusted Christians who might be able to direct you to a group of people working through issues of sexual abuse. In *Healing from Sexual Abuse,* the author, known only as Kathleen, shares her journey of recovery.

> Then I knew. The floodgates opened. The pain engulfed me. I couldn't run anywhere to hide. I felt paralyzed. Never in my life had anything hurt this much. The entire buried trauma came to the surface. I felt caught in a wave of pain, and I couldn't see my way clear. . . . I sat numbed and dazed in my favorite rocking chair. Snuggled in an afghan, I kept thinking, "Is this pain ever going to end, or will I always hurt this much?"
>
> Then the words of Jeremiah came to me, "For I know the plans I have for you," says the Lord, "plans for welfare and not for evil, to give you a future and a hope" Jeremiah 29:11 (RSV). I clung to those words. They became my lifeline. I called Sharon, a Christian therapist, and asked for an appointment. I couldn't recover alone. I needed help. I'll always remember the first words she said on the phone. "I guess you're ready to work on this now." These nine little words brought me hope. Yes, I was ready. Sexual abuse victims fear the pain of remembering. They assume the pain will never leave them. The truth is that remembering is the only way to move through the pain into acceptance. Incest is a crime of secrecy—victims have been told not to tell anyone what transpired in their home. But to move into recovery, the victim needs to break the bonds of secrecy and tell her (his) story.[19]

Perhaps the most damaging part of sexual abuse is the distortions it teaches us about sex. Instead of seeing sex as God's good gift given to a husband and wife in a loving relationship, sexual abuse hijacks sex and turns it into an ugly and selfish distortion.

Romans 12:1-2 says, "Therefore, I urge you, brothers and sisters, in view of God's mercy, to offer your bodies as a living sacrifice, holy and pleasing to God—this is true worship. Do not conform to the pattern of this world, but be transformed by the renewing of your mind. Then you will be able to test and approve what God's will is— his good, pleasing and perfect will." I love the way this verse brings out the fact that our bodies belong to God. They are living sacrifices, holy and pleasing to God.

Did you catch that? Our bodies are a holy sacrifice, pleasing to God. He desires that we give them to him as an act of worship. When Christ died on the cross, he died for everything in the world that isn't right. As we come to the cross of Jesus, we can find healing and a redeemed view of our bodies. His blood will wash away any sin that we've committed and any sin committed against us. We emerge with a holy body, cleansed and ready to be offered to God.

God removes our guilt and our shame. Guilt is tied to wrongdoing and says, "I have done something wrong" but shame is a pervasive feeling that says, "I'm hopelessly flawed and defective." God wants to take away both our guilt and shame.

Romans 12:2 goes on to talk about being transformed by renewing our minds. Much of the work of recovering from sexual abuse is rejecting the lies we believe and embracing the truth of God. We're not dirty or spoiled. We each are precious daughters and sons of the living God and stand before him clothed in the righteousness of Christ.

Wendy Maltz, a therapist who works extensively with sexual abuse victims, has come up with a helpful chart contrasting unhealthy sexual attitudes with healthy sexual attitudes:[20]

Unhealthy Sexual Attitudes	Healthy Sexual Attitudes
Sex is evil.	Sex is a gift from God.
Sex is an obligation.	Sex is a choice.
Sex is addictive.	Sex is a natural drive.
Sex is hurtful.	Sex is nurturing, healing.
Sex is a condition for receiving love.	Sex is an expression of love.
Sex is secretive.	Sex is private.
Sex is exploitive.	Sex is mutual.
Sex benefits one person.	Sex is respectful.
Sex is unsafe.	Sex is safe.
Sex is power over someone.	Sex is empowering.

Perhaps as you read through the two lists, you found yourself with a combination of attitudes, some unhealthy and some healthy. As you pray for God's healing, ask him to reprogram your mind with the healthy sexual attitudes. Ask him to help you view yourself, sexuality, sex, men and women through his eyes.

If you're dating seriously, it's good to share about your sexual abuse with him or her. Your partner will be far more understanding if you flinch at casual physical contact knowing you've been traumatized. A loving partner can be used by God in powerful ways to heal you and reprogram your thinking about the gift of sex. If you've been sexually abused, you *can* have a good sex life in marriage with God's healing and help.[21]

14 Why are relationships so messed up these days?

If God thought up sex, and it's such a wonderful gift to men and women, why are relationships so messed up? Why are there broken relationships, date rape victims, girlfriends who cheat on their boyfriends, boyfriends who cheat on their girlfriends and abusive relationships?

THE WAY THINGS WERE SUPPOSED TO BE

God is the creator of the galaxies, animals, plants and human beings. Our fundamental understanding of ourselves is that we are the creation of God.

> Then God said, "Let us make human beings in our image, in our likeness, so that they may rule over the fish in the sea and the birds in the sky, over the livestock and all the wild animals, and over all the creatures that move along the ground." So God created human beings in his own image, in the image of God he created them; male and female he created them. God blessed them and said to them, "Be fruitful and increase in number; fill the earth and subdue it. Rule over the fish in the sea and the birds in the sky and over every living creature that moves on the ground." (Genesis 1:26-28)

You and I can never make sense of our lives apart from knowing that we are the magnificent workmanship of God created in his image. That means that we are moral beings with a sense of right and wrong; we are word partners with God and can accumulate knowledge over time; we can create. It means we have emotions and can feel deeply.

Notice that both the man and the woman were told, "Be fruitful and increase in number; fill the earth and subdue it." God's intention is that the task of bearing and raising children be done in the community of a husband and wife living together in loving unity for a lifetime.

Also, they were commanded to rule over God's creation and have dominion over the earth. Sometimes people have mistakenly taken these two tasks and given the be-fruitful-and-multiply part to women and the rule-over-the-earth part to men. God gave both of these commands to both people. He intended that they work together in loving cooperation to accomplish these two great tasks.

In the creation account, whenever God created something, he proclaimed that it was good. But in Genesis 2:18, this pattern was broken. "It is *not good* for the man to be alone." Adam was in a perfect environment having fellowship with a perfect God, yet something was not good: the aloneness of Adam was not good.

Genesis 2 gives us a close-up look at the creation of Eve. Genesis 2:18-25 says,

> The LORD God said, "It is not good for the man to be alone. I will make a helper suitable for him." Now the LORD God had formed out of the ground all the wild animals and all the birds in the sky. He brought them to the man to see what he would name them; and whatever the man called each living creature, that was its name. So the man gave names to all the livestock, the birds in the sky and all the wild animals. But for Adam no suitable helper was found. So the LORD God caused the man to fall into a deep sleep; and while he was sleeping, he took one of the man's ribs and then closed up the place with flesh. Then the LORD God made a woman from the rib he had taken out of the

man, and he brought her to the man. The man said, "This is
now bone of my bones and flesh of my flesh; she shall be called
'woman,' for she was taken out of man." For this reason a man
will leave his father and mother and be united to his wife, and
they will become one flesh. The man and his wife were both naked, and they felt no shame.

When God created Eve, he addressed Adam's aloneness by creating a wife for him. In addition, God created community. You may
have heard the expression that people have a God-shaped vacuum in
their hearts, but they also have a people-shaped vacuum in their
hearts. God intends for us to live in the company of people. From this
text we can see that we need each other and that people are a gift
from God to remedy our aloneness.

The phrase that describes Eve, a "helper suitable for him," contains two Hebrew words. The first word, *ezer,* is used as the noun *help*
or *helper* and appears twenty-one times in the Old Testament. Sometimes this term is used to refer to God, such as in Psalm 121:1-2: "I
lift up my eyes to the mountains—where does my help come from?
My help comes from the LORD, the Maker of heaven and earth." *Ezer*
refers to a superior helper, such as God, sixteen times and to an equal
five times. It never refers to a subordinate helper unless Genesis 2 is
the only exception. The word *help* or *helper* is a wonderfully rich Hebrew word that means one who comes to the rescue of another or one
who brings resources.

It's important to understand this Hebrew word because some
Christians have mistakenly taken this verse to imply women's inferi-
ority of value or rank. The accurate understanding is that Adam
found in Eve an equal partner who brought resources to him.

The second word is *neged,* a Hebrew word that means suitable, perfectly complementary. This is a reference to their anatomy, but even more so to Eve's ability to round out Adam's personality. If the world was only filled with men, something of God would be missing. If the world was only filled with women, something of God would be missing. It takes both men and women together to accurately reflect the image of God.

Before God created the woman, all the animals were brought before Adam, and he had the task of naming them. I can imagine Adam laughing at the hippo and marveling at the giraffe, but despite his delights, he realized that he had no counterpart. The animals only underscored his aloneness.

God put Adam into a deep sleep, and when he awoke, his blurry eyes beheld a naked woman! I am sure he looked at her and immediately realized that she was his counterpart. She was unlike the animals. She was a human being like he was. He must have thought, *She is like me! She has arms and legs like me, yet she is delightfully different! She has skin like me, but her skin is so soft. She has breasts like me, but hers are different!*

Finally, Adam had a partner. We sense the sheer ecstasy they felt in one another. As Adam and Eve gazed at each other, they knew they belonged to one another. They were fascinated by the fact that they were alike but also wonderfully different.

There was no sense of comparison. Because Eve didn't get *Glamour* magazine, if her breasts were small, she didn't know it. If Adam didn't have washboard abs, he didn't know it. There wasn't an ex lurking in the shadowy background. They were naked and unashamed. This magnetic attraction of soul and body was to continue to pull them back into one another's arms. They found in one another a best friend to share the joys and sorrows of life.

We yearn to return to this Genesis 2 moment. A husband and wife should find in each other a companion with whom they can be naked and unashamed. They are drawn to each other through love and sexual attraction. And there exists a profound sense that "you were made for me. You complete me. You're made by God, and you're God's gift to me."

THINGS FALL APART

I wish we could freeze time at the point where Adam and Eve are enjoying the transparent, shameless connection in the Garden of Eden. But in the next chapter of Genesis, we encounter what theologians call the Fall. In Genesis 3, Eve, deceived by the serpent, disobeys God and eats from a tree that was off limits to her. She invites Adam to join her in this rebellion, and he also eats from the forbidden tree.

Sin is let loose in the world and as a result, everything is messed up. Their relationships with God are broken, their relationship with each other is broken, and even the environment is marred.

> When the woman saw that the fruit of the tree was good for food and pleasing to the eye, and also desirable for gaining wisdom, she took some and ate it. She also gave some to her husband, who was with her, and he ate it. Then the eyes of both of them were opened, and they realized they were naked; so they sewed fig leaves together and made coverings for themselves.
>
> Then the man and his wife heard the sound of the LORD God as he was walking in the garden in the cool of the day, and they hid from the LORD God among the trees of the garden. But the LORD God called to the man, "Where are you?" (Genesis 3:6-9)

Before they were naked and unashamed; now they're hiding from one another and from God. They sewed fig leaves and covered themselves up. Shame is the intruder into their hearts. I've heard it said that the whole Bible can be summed up in one tiny phrase, when God was calling to Adam: "Where are you?" God, in love, pursues sinners.

God also pronounced curses on the serpent, the woman and the man. Sin has destructive effects. Genesis 3:16 reads, "To the woman he said, 'I will make your pains in childbearing very severe; with pain you will give birth to children. Your desire will be for your husband, and he will rule over you.'"

The phrase, "Your desire will be for your husband," means that she will turn away from God as her primary love relationship and look to her husband to meet the deepest needs of her soul. Unfortunately, many women are deeply disappointed with marriage because they expect their husbands to meet needs that only God can meet.

The last part of this verse, "Your desire will be for your husband, and he will rule over you" has presented a fork in the road for Christians through the ages. There are two ways that this verse can be taken.

- "He will rule over you" is understood to be an expression of God's will. Eve must realize that because of the Fall she's now in a place of subordination under Adam, and this is God's will for her.

- "He will rule over you" is understood to be a prophetic statement of what would happen when sin was let loose in the world. It is a prediction of an event that will happen, like when Jesus says in John 13:38, "Peter, before the rooster crows, you will disown me three times." Jesus is not giving Peter a command but, rather, is making a prediction of something that will take place in the future. The verb tense used ("will rule") is not an imperative (command); rather it is a Hebrew imperfect, usually translated as a future or present verb.

Both interpretations take the biblical text seriously and consider it as God's sacred Word, but each interpretation will take you to radically different views of the marriage relationship. If you go with the first interpretation, you'll see the many curses spoken to the serpent and to Eve and to Adam as an expression of God's will and something to be enforced for all of eternity. This interpretation explains why years ago, women were forbidden to use painkillers in childbirth. Theologians wanted to stay true to the literal understanding of "with pain you will give birth to children." They reasoned that women's punishment for sin was pain in childbirth and to alleviate this pain was resisting the will of God.[22]

If the phrase "he will rule over you" is taken to be prescriptive and not descriptive (the first view), then to be entirely consistent, we must also enforce the curses given to men. The parallel construction of these statements won't allow us to view one as an expression of God's perfect will and the other as an obstacle to overcome with God's grace.

The second interpretation, which I think is correct, sees the dominion of men not as a statement of God's will but a prediction of what would happen as a result of sin being let loose in the world. The harmony between men and women would be replaced by domination and exploitation of women.

The entire list of negative predictions can be overcome by the power of Christ, who came not only to redeem lost humanity but also to reverse the negative effects of the Fall.

A look at history will show us how completely this prophecy has been fulfilled. If we look at places in the world where women are the most repressed, we notice that they are places where the gospel of Christ has not penetrated. The message of Christ has elevated the status of women wherever the gospel is received.

In summary, God created men and women to be complementary. Together they carry out the mandate to be fruitful, multiply and fill the earth and to have dominion over the earth. Unfortunately, when Adam and Eve chose to disobey God, sin was let loose in the world. As a result, everything got messed up. When we see exploitation, rape, incest, adultery, sexual abuse and broken relationships, we realize these are byproducts of the Fall. That's why relationships are so messed up. Only through Jesus Christ can things be set right.

15 My friend struggles with homosexuality. What should I do?

Henry began leading a Bible study during his sophomore year for guys on his dorm floor. Each Wednesday night at nine his tiny room was jammed with twelve guys. Two guys perched atop bunk beds, one sat on the dorm fridge, six were sprawled on the floor, two were seated on the windowsill and one raging extrovert sat on a bicycle. Discussions were lively, and the debates often continued way past the appointed finishing time.

Henry had attended a week of Bible study leader's training and felt like things were going along as planned. That is, until one night when Jared opened up about struggling with homosexuality. Hmm, the Bible study leader's training had not covered that.

Henry had read a little about homosexuality and had been in on some campus discussions about gay rights, but suddenly this topic had a name and a face: Jared.

I told Henry what pains me is the way the Christian church has often treated homosexual people. We often turn a blind eye toward the unmarried heterosexual couple sleeping together and shun the person who is gay. Many Christians are deeply concerned about the gay agenda attacking our concept of family, but even greater damage is being done by heterosexuals who divorce. When my husband was a pastor in Ann Arbor, Michigan, a man drove over one hundred miles to meet with him because he said my husband had a reputation of teaching biblical truth and being loving toward homosexual people.

INFLUENCING FACTORS

What causes homosexual desires? Stanton L. Jones describes the influencing factors in *The Gay Debate:* "The evidence suggests that genetic factors, possibly operative through brain differences, may give some a push in the direction of homosexual preferences. Disordered family relationships that leave people confused and uncertain at a deep level about their sexual identity seem to play a major role as well. Early homosexual experiences of seduction or abuse may also play a role. And many lesbians, especially, seem to have been the targets of sexual abuse by men early in life, leaving them with deeply impaired abilities to trust or feel close to men."[23]

When Jared shared with Henry about his homosexual desires he reasoned, "If I have a strong desire for something, it must have been put there by God. If God put it there, then he would want me to have that desire fulfilled." Henry wasn't so sure about this. Should a person seek to fulfill all their strong desires?

We must remember the human heart is a cauldron of desires—some so noble we feel like kindred spirits to Mother Teresa and others so base we dare not share them with our dearest friend. Giving full reign to our strong desires could lead us to have extramarital affairs, drink excessively, embezzle money at work, become violent with idiots on the highway and tell off our annoying aunt. Surely desires must be sifted and sorted. Not all strong desires can find expression. All people—gay and straight—are a mixture of noble and base desires.

What does the Bible say about homosexuality? The biblical texts of the Old Testament that condemn homosexual acts are Leviticus 18:22 and 20:13, Deuteronomy 23:18, and Genesis 19:1-29. Many have argued that the New Testament is about love and inclusiveness so we can disregard these Old Testament admonitions.

But the New Testament also denounces homosexual practices. Romans 1:18-32 states that homosexual practices are not acceptable. Although the Bible spans hundreds of years and many cultures, every time homosexual acts are mentioned in the Bible, they are condemned. One passage that is extremely instructive is 1 Corinthians 6:9-11. The apostle Paul writes, "Do you not know that wrongdoers will not inherit the kingdom of God? Do not be deceived: Neither the sexually immoral nor idolaters nor adulterers nor male prostitutes nor practicing homosexuals nor thieves nor the greedy nor drunkards nor slanderers nor swindlers will inherit the kingdom of God. And that is what some of you were. But you were washed, you were sanctified, you were justified in the name of the Lord Jesus Christ and by the Spirit of our God."

Paul rattles off a litany of sins, things unacceptable to God. Homosexual offenders are on that list. But notice that homosexual people are right next to slanderers, drunkards and greedy people. It's hard to read through that list and not see yourself. Even if you've never been a homosexual offender, greed and slander nail us. "But that is what some of you *were*." Past tense. These sinners have been redeemed and now comprise the church of Corinth.

It's important to distinguish between homosexual desires and homosexual acts. We cannot be held accountable for our longings or our temptations, but we can be held accountable for our behavior. There are many people who find themselves with homosexual desires but choose not to act on them because of their faith in Christ and a conviction that sexual activity between two people of the same sex is outside God's will.

Let's face it. We wrestle with temptation our whole lives. Our struggle with the flesh never ends. To be human is to find that our natural inclinations war against God's standards. Even Jesus wrestled with temptation (Luke 4:1-13) and yet we know that Jesus was sinless. The life of Jesus teaches us more about how to live with unmet longings than about how to get our needs met.

British scholar Amy Orr-Ewing writes, "The Christian would want to affirm the dignity of every human being and make a distinction between personhood and behavior. This is why it's possible for a Christian to say that homosexual activity is wrong, but people who have homosexual orientation are loved and welcomed. For a Christian, identity does not come from what I do, whether that be vocational or sexual; my identity is rooted in being a child of God. What I do then flows from that."[24]

CHANGE IS POSSIBLE

Great debates have raged over whether a person's sexual orientation is fixed or changeable. Amy Orr-Ewing writes about Dr. Spitzer, professor of psychiatry at Columbia University, New York, and his research:

> He is well known for having been instrumental in deleting homosexuality from the American Psychiatric Association's list of mental disorders in 1973. His recent study has caused uproar by suggesting that homosexuals can change their sexuality. He

found that 78 percent of males and 95 percent of females who voluntarily underwent "reparative" or psychiatric therapy reported a change in their sexuality. Of the 143 men and 57 women who participated, 66 percent of males and 44 percent of females had achieved what he called "good heterosexual functioning." This study has been vociferously criticized because many of the participants expressed the fact that their Christian faith had helped them. The research has been decried as "fundamentalist" and "bogus." However, Dr. Spitzer describes himself as an "atheist Jew" whose interest is in scientific truth. He writes, "My conclusion is that the door is open. . . . . I came to this study as a skeptic—I believed that a homosexual, whether born or made, was a homosexual and that to consider their orientation a matter of choice was wrong. But the fact is that if I found even one person who could change, the door is open and a change in sexual orientation is possible.[25]

My own experience with lesbians and gay men has shown that some people can and do change their sexual orientation. Some of the homosexual people I met with years ago are married today after they changed their orientation. Other gay people have not changed and continue to be attracted to same-sex relationships. For them God's grace came not in a change of orientation but in the ability to live as celibate single people with unmet longings.

CONVICTION PLUS GRACE

The challenge of the church today is to figure out how to uphold biblical convictions, yet do so in a grace-filled way. Homophobia is the hatred of homosexual people, but that must be seen as different from disapproving of homosexual practice for biblical reasons.

As Christians, we need to create a safe place where people can open up and be known and loved. When abuse and neglect have left people broken (straight or gay), the church should be the place to experience wholesome family love as God intended. Our family has often adopted hurting people. Having them join us in making homemade pizza, hiking with the kids and the dog, and just talking over coffee can be healing. The greatest damage to people occurs in relationships, but the greatest healing of people occurs in relationships. Maybe Christians wouldn't be labeled homophobic if we upheld our biblical convictions with humility and a vulnerability that shares our own brokenness and our own suffering.

A BAND OF BROTHERS

The teaching of the Bible is a call to disciplined fidelity between one man and one woman in marriage. And for everyone who isn't married, the call is to celibacy and chastity. Henry and the guys in the dorm Bible study, presumably single, are called to purity. More than likely, some of the guys in Henry's Bible study are fighting addiction to pornography and some are struggling to keep a lid on sexual activity with their girlfriends. Straight or gay, these men need to see themselves as fellow strugglers in a corporate quest for holiness. These men need to band together to offer one another a counterculture that stands against the voices that say, "You're not a real man unless you're sexually active." Small groups provide a great place to pursue holiness in the company of friends who hold each other accountable and offer grace and prayer if and when they fail.

16 What if I don't feel guilty when I have sex?

What if my boyfriend and I don't feel guilty when we have sex? For us it's a wonderful time of closely connecting." This question was scribbled on an index card and submitted for a panel discussion's Q and A time.

The student who wrote this question had heard a lot of Christian teaching on the dangers of premarital sex. She had been told that premarital sex is a damaging experience and is followed by horrible feelings of regret and shame. But that simply had not been her experience. She had found sexual intercourse to be a wonderful time of closely connecting with her boyfriend, and the tenderness they shared simply did not accord with the terrible experiences mentioned by Christian speakers.

Many people are eaten up with guilt after having premarital sex, feeling empty and remorseful, but many people aren't. They report feelings of closeness being deeply loved.

An old adage says, "Let your conscience be your guide." At first glance this may seem like a good guideline, but unfortunately it does not take into account how malformed our consciences can be.

This truth is clearly seen in the case of the murderer who has strangled four victims yet feels no guilt or remorse. For a less extreme case, think of your own friends who steal and have no guilt. The conscience has holes in it. Conversely, think of the pastor who feels guilty because he cannot personally invite all eight hundred people in his congregation over for dinner at his home during the year. Sometimes we feel guilty for things that aren't wrong. That is false guilt.

Why are our consciences so screwed up? We're fallen. In Genesis 3, Adam and Eve chose to disobey God and as a result, sin was let loose in the world and everything got messed up: the environment, our relationships and even our sense of right and wrong. It's the nature of sin to whisper lies into our ears. Satan is called the father of lies, and he deceives us. He makes us feel that we are missing out, that God is withholding good from us. He convinces us that bad things are really good and that good things are bad. Our feelings are important and must be listened to, but they cannot be our ultimate guide.

I have a friend who teaches flying at an aviation school. One of the most important lessons for pilots to learn is to read and trust the instrument panel. In the cockpit are a zillion switches, lights and gadgets that each indicate important information. While flying, pilots can lose their sense of direction, even which way is up, so they must learn to trust what the instrument panels says in spite of what feels right. This is a good analogy for us. We must trust in the Bible and God's revealed truth more than our own feelings of right and wrong.

We also must be careful not to tell people what feelings they will have. Our credibility plummets when we make an assertion that another person finds untrue. So Christian teaching on sexuality should not insist that everybody will always have regrets after premarital sex. Lauren F. Winner states this well in *Real Sex:*

> To insist that people will feel terrible after premarital sex is not only to miss something essential about the way sin's deceptions work, it is also to make a pastoral faux pas. Let's imagine Lillian, a young woman who has heard since puberty that premarital sex will leave her feeling guilt-ridden and lonely. For years, she avoids temptation, but she's come to her mid twenties, she's not married, she's been dating the same guy for eight months, and eventually, she has sex. Perhaps she will feel horrible, but per-

haps she won't. And then Lillian may think 'Hmmmm, My pastor has been telling me for a decade that this would feel bad, but it doesn't. Maybe everything else he told me about sex is wrong too.' If guilt is the only resource the church has given Lillian to diagnose sin and remain chaste, in the absence of guilt, she will simply keep having sex, not to mention she'll begin to doubt the authority of her pastor."[26]

It's fair to say that sometimes our consciences are malformed. Feeling guilty or not feeling guilty is a poor guide to moral choices. Thankfully God has given us commands and guidelines to live by. In time, his wisdom and love will be shown true.

17 What's so bad about being friends with benefits and hooking up?

The term "hooking up" refers to two people who seek the pleasure of sex apart from any relationship. Hooking up can mean kissing, oral sex or intercourse. *Friends with benefits* is hooking up with a friend on a regular basis. This practice is common on college campuses and among high school students.

The *New York Times* published "Friends, Friends with Benefits and the Benefits of the Local Mall" by Benoit Denizet-Lewis. After countless interviews with teenagers, the author concludes,

To a generation raised on MTV, AIDS, Britney Spears, Internet porn, Monica Lewinsky and "Sex in the City," oral sex is definitely not sex and hooking up is definitely not a big deal. The teenagers I spoke to talk about hookups as matter-of-factly as they might discuss what's on the cafeteria lunch menu—and they look at you in a funny way if you go on for too long about the "emotional" components of sex.[27]

In this same article, a girl named Irene was interviewed and spelled out the unwritten etiquette of hooking up:

> If you want to be in a hookup relationship, then you don't call the person for anything except plans to hook up. You don't invite them out with you. You don't call just to say hi. You don't confuse the matter. You just keep it purely sexual, and that way people don't have mixed expectations, and no one gets hurt.

Sexual activity outside the bonds of marriage is as old as time. What *is* new is the open acceptance of sexual activity void of any relationship. People are looking for the pleasure of sex, without the complications of a relationship.

WHY PEOPLE HOOK UP

Here are a handful of reasons why people choose to hook up.

- Many high school and college students know they have years of education ahead of them and don't want to become emotionally entangled by being in a relationship. With no hope of marriage in the near future, hooking up is a way to enjoy the pleasures of sex now.

  I spoke with a college student who said, "I have a 'friends with benefits' relationship with a guy I know from class. I have two more years of college and then three years of grad school ahead of me. I don't want a relationship with anyone right now. Falling in love and getting married would derail me from my career path."

- Relationships and dating take time and money. In this fast-paced world, hooking up can save the time and money one might spend on dinner and a movie. The pair sets a time and place for sexual encounters and then they get back to life: homework, employment, committee meetings and e-mail.

- In the wake of broken romances, many people feel that it's safer to not become emotionally involved. They're willing to give their body away, but not their hearts. They've chosen to disconnect: If I don't expect any relationship then I can't be disappointed. Caring for the person you have sex with is seen as being needy. Some people who hook up boast that they can have a sexual encounter and not fall in love.

- Some women, tired of the double standard, reason that if it's okay for guys to play the field and have numerous sex partners without commitment, they can too. Things are more equitable if men use women and women use men—or so the reasoning goes.

I met weekly with Stephanie, who was in the habit of going to bars and hooking up. I asked her to share with me what she was thinking and feeling during these hookups. She said, "Some guy comes up to me at a bar and wants to buy me a shot. He wants to put his arm around me and kiss me. And I think 'Wow, out of all the girls in the bar, he chose me!' It makes me feel special to be pursued. And then when we go back to his place or mine, for a little while I feel truly loved." Stephanie knew these guys would never call her, and she was fine with that. The intoxicating feeling of being chosen, pursued and loved—even for a fleeting moment—was addictive. She was using her sexual powers to gain a feeling of significance.

Later I asked Stephanie, "What if a man pursued you and loved you for a lifetime? What if he was faithful to you and wanted to get to know the real you? Would you want to be married and have sex with someone like that?" Stephanie looked down and said softly, "Sure, but that's as likely as me winning the lottery and my divorced parents getting remarried." She knew she was settling for a counterfeit, but it was all her heart could hope for.

What might be going on inside a guy who's hooking up? While serving at a student camp in Michigan, I met a good-looking guy named José. He had recently come to faith in Christ. He told me he was struggling to give up his lifestyle of hooking up. He said, "I'm known as a player. Girls love me. I work out, and I wear clothes that show off what I've got. Knowing that some girl wants me lights me up on the inside. Getting her to go to bed with me makes me feel powerful. How can I ever give that up? That's who I am!"

For both Stephanie and José, the testing and proving of their sexual powers was the fuel they ran on.

THE BODY AND SOUL UNITED

Hooking up and friends with benefits rests on the belief that what we do with our bodies is somehow disconnected from who we are. But the truth is we are a union of body, soul and spirit. We cannot segment a human being into parts. This false view that God only cares about the spirit and doesn't care about the body was one of the heresies of the early church. The apostle Paul addressed this when he wrote,

> The body, however, is not meant for sexual immorality but for the Lord, and the Lord for the body. By his power God raised the Lord from the dead, and he will raise us also. Do you not know that your bodies are members of Christ himself? Shall I then take the members of Christ and unite them with a prostitute? Never! Do you not know that he who unites himself with

a prostitute is one with her in body? For it is said, "The two will become one flesh." But whoever is united with the Lord is one with him in spirit.

Flee from sexual immorality. All other sins people commit are outside their bodies, but those who sin sexually sin against their own bodies. Do you not know that your bodies are temples of the Holy Spirit, who is in you, whom you have received from God? You are not your own; you were bought at a price. Therefore honor God with your bodies. (1 Corinthians 6:13-20)

Hooking up is self-destructive and leaves us broken. Over time it erodes our sense of self-worth and causes emotional and relational damage. If we train ourselves to be emotionally and relationally numb during sex, it can be difficult to reconnect our heart, soul and body. God's plan is that we give ourselves bodies, souls and spirits to one person in marriage. In this safe and lifelong commitment, sex finds its full expression

Is it realistic to assume that people can easily switch from hooking up to a stable monogamous marriage? Frequent hookups create an appetite for the exhilaration of sex with someone new. People are in essence programming themselves for infidelity. They come to see people as interchangeable sources of sexual pleasure. The buzz is in the new conquest.

Also consider the ramifications of marrying someone who has had numerous hookups. Do you want to be compared to a string of former lovers? You may get the feeling that your marriage partner is coaching you to replicate the pleasure of a former hookup.

In John 12:3, Mary poured expensive perfume on Jesus' feet. The perfume was of such great value that some of those watching were appalled at the extravagance of the gift. I often think of my sexuality as being like the expensive perfume that Mary poured on Jesus' feet. My sexuality is precious; I'm lavishly spending it on one lucky man— my husband, Bill.

Whether you're male or female, treasure your sexuality. Realize that your sexuality is far more than external organs. Your sexuality penetrates to the deepest core of who you are. Being male or being female means that you possess a unique way to touch the soul of another human being. Don't squander your sexual powers, doling it out in pieces to random partners. Think of saving it to spend lavishly on one lucky person—your marriage partner.

18 I feel like damaged goods. Who will ever want me?

My cell phone had a desperate message from Paige: "Can you meet with my friend Karli? She's in utter despair, and I don't have a clue what to say to her. She needs to talk with someone like you."

I set up a time to meet with Karli in a quiet coffee shop. After exchanging brief biographies, she stopped talking and looked down. In silence Karli began twisting a paper napkin. Tears began rolling down her cheeks. She stammered, "I've messed up. A few days ago I found out that I have an STD, and when I told my boyfriend, he broke up with me immediately. I feel like damaged goods. Who will ever want me?"

Karli was in anguish over the news of her sexually transmitted disease, but more upsetting was the reaction of her boyfriend; he only confirmed her worst fears. Karli's openness with me allowed us to talk at length about her medical condition, about the loss of this guy she thought she was in love with and about her sense of feeling dirty. Most people feel guilty when they mess up, but somehow, sexual failure runs much deeper. They not only feel guilt, but they feel shame. Sexual sin often leaves people feeling dirty. The depth of this guilt and shame is paradoxically a validation that God's original design for sex is good.

As Karli and I met weekly, I found out that she had gone to church a few times in her childhood, but God wasn't a part of her life. Before this crisis she had no interest in God, but now she sensed that if there were a God, he would be frowning at her.

I told Karli that Jesus had many encounters with people who failed sexually. He seemed to understand the depth of their pain and met them with compassion and forgiveness. Actually Jesus' harshest words were not for the sexually promiscuous, but for the prideful.

Jesus told a story about a religious leader (a Pharisee) and a tax collector, who by occupation was considered to be a crooked, greedy sellout.

To some who were confident of their own righteousness and looked down on everyone else, Jesus told this parable: "Two men went up to the temple to pray, one a Pharisee and the other a tax collector. The Pharisee stood by himself and prayed: 'God, I thank you that I am not like other people—robbers, evildoers, adulterers—or even like this tax collector. I fast twice a week and give a tenth of all I get.'

"But the tax collector stood at a distance. He would not even look up to heaven, but beat his breast and said, 'God have mercy on me, a sinner.'

"I tell you that this man, rather than the other, went home justified before God. For all those who exalt themselves will be

humbled, and those who humble themselves will be exalted."
(Luke 18:9-14)

Feeling broken and spiritually unworthy, like the tax collector, or like
Karli, is the first step to experiencing the grace and forgiveness of
God.

FINDING FORGIVENESS

In the coffee shop I also shared with Karli an encounter Jesus had
with a woman caught in the act of adultery. I wanted her to see Jesus
as the source of forgiveness and new beginnings.

> But Jesus went to the Mount of Olives. At dawn he appeared
> again in the temple courts, where all the people gathered
> around him, and he sat down to teach them. The teachers of the
> law and the Pharisees brought in a woman caught in adultery.
> They made her stand before the group and said to Jesus,
> "Teacher, this woman was caught in the act of adultery. In the
> Law Moses commanded us to stone such women. Now what do
> you say?" They were using this question as a trap, in order to
> have a basis for accusing him.
>
> But Jesus bent down and started to write on the ground with
> his finger. When they kept on questioning him, he straightened
> up and said to them, "Let any one of you who is without sin be
> the first to throw a stone at her." Again he stooped down and
> wrote on the ground.
>
> At this, those who heard began to go away one at a time, the
> older ones first, until only Jesus was left, with the woman still
> standing there. Jesus straightened up and asked her, "Woman,
> where are they? Has no one condemned you?"

"No one, sir," she said.

"Then neither do I condemn you," declared Jesus. "Go now and leave your life of sin." (John 8:1-11)

It's hard to imagine the depth of shame this woman must have felt. Jewish law required witnesses who had actually seen the act of adultery occurring. Suspicion and hearsay were not sufficient evidence to accuse. To have men bust in during a moment of sexual passion, force her to come to the temple, the holiest place in town, and then force her to stand in front of Jesus and a crowd of people was a most horrible situation. This was a small town where everybody knew everybody. Was she partially clothed? Was she wrapped in a bed sheet? Was her mom or dad in the crowd? Her brothers or sisters? Her children? Her husband?

The Jewish law required that both the man and the woman caught in the act of adultery be stoned (Leviticus 20:10; Deuteronomy 22:22). In this situation they let the man go free; the woman alone was called to account. The injustice of their "justice" is infuriating.

She must have known that she was a pawn. The men who brought her to the temple didn't care about her sexual purity; they were using her to trap Jesus. The Roman government did not allow the Jews to carry out death sentences, so if Jesus had given permission to stone her, he would have been in conflict with the Romans. If he had let her go free, he would be accused of not upholding Jewish law.

But Jesus outfoxed them. He said, "Let any one of you who is without sin be the first to throw a stone at her." I have often wondered what he wrote on the ground. Was it something like *last summer with Rebekah?* Whatever it was, it uncovered their sin. It laid bare their self-righteous hypocrisy. One by one they left. Only Jesus was left with her.

NEITHER DO I CONDEMN YOU

When you think about it, the person who was without sin was Jesus. He should have cast the first stone at her—but he didn't. Jesus asked her where her accusers were. He underscored the fact that the ugly crowd of accusers was silenced. Their mouths were shut. Then he uttered the most wonderful words her ears would ever hear, "Neither do I condemn you. Go now and leave your life of sin."

What a day it had been for her. Jesus, the perfect, holy one, the great teacher, the one who should have cast the first stone did not condemn her. Instead he set her free, to go without condemnation, to leave her life of sin.

I asked Karli to put herself into this story, to see herself standing alone with Jesus, overwhelmed by shame, expecting condemnation, only to hear the words of Jesus, words spoken to her: "Where are they? Has no one condemned you? Neither do I condemn you. Go now and leave your life of sin." This was a different Jesus than Karli had known. Again Karli's eyes were cast down. It was almost too good to believe.

The words of Jesus are powerful. They are life altering. Jesus has the power to remove all our guilt and shame and to heal our brokenness. When Jesus died on the cross, a great exchange happened. As the perfect man he took upon himself all our sins, sexual sins and every other kind, and endured the punishment that should have been ours. And then he transferred his righteousness to us. Slowly this great theological truth began to seep into Karli's broken heart. She began to see herself as forgiven, cleansed and clothed in the righteousness of Christ.

Jesus not only forgives us, but he sets us free to begin a new life. I wish I could read the sequel to the story of the woman brought to

Jesus. What happened when she left Jesus at that moment? Who did she become? What did her life look like ten years later, twenty years later? I expect that her life was transformed by her encounter with Christ.

I do know what happened to Karli. It was a pleasure to watch her life change over the course of the semester. She became a Christian, drinking in the love and forgiveness of Christ. Karli never got back together with her former boyfriend, but God began to fill her life with rich relationships. Her friend Paige became a big sister to her and helped her become grafted into the Christian community on campus. Karli attended a weeklong Christian camp at the end of the school year, and I smiled inside when I saw her canoeing, hiking and hanging out with a great group of friends.

God gave Karli an unexpected gift of encouragement. Soon after Karli became a Christian, she decided to reconnect with an old friend she had known in high school. He was a committed Christian, and she knew he would be glad to hear of her newfound faith in Christ. They reconnected through e-mail and in one e-mail, this guy she thought of as a spiritual superstar confided that at one time he feared he had gotten his girlfriend pregnant. After the pregnancy scare, he and his girlfriend backed up on their physical involvement and sought to have a sexually pure relationship. Knowing this guy's story of sexual failure and restoration, yet respecting him deeply, allowed Karli to believe that it's possible to respect someone with a sinful past. She realized that she and this high school friend stood on level ground, at the foot of the cross of Christ.

If you're not a follower of Christ, you can become one now. Your new life can begin today. He has wonderful things in store for you, if you'll just entrust yourself to him. You can begin a personal relationship with Christ by saying a simple prayer, something like this: "Jesus forgive me. Thank you for dying on the cross to pay for my sins. Wash me clean. I give myself to you, body, soul and mind. Lead me and show me the wonderful plans you have for my life. Amen."

As you begin this new relationship realize that you're not intended to live the Christian life in isolation. Like Karli, you need to connect with a community of believers who will share your beliefs and provide you with the opportunity to have deep and meaning friendships—plus a fun social life.

THE PRODIGAL

If you're a Christian and have failed sexually, you can get back on track with God. Maybe you had a vital faith in days past but for whatever reason you've wandered off the path of God and are not sure how you got where you are.

Lamar was a kid who grew up in church. Even though his mom worked two jobs she was there whenever the sanctuary doors opened, always wearing a fancy hat. As a little boy, Lamar's favorite part of church was the choir. They would sway in shimmering robes, belting out gospel tunes with Willie, a heavyset man, improvising on the organ. Lamar always had a warm feeling of being in the presence of a holy God even when he fell asleep on the blue velvet pew cushions. But when Lamar got to middle school, Sunday church with mom seemed disconnected from the rest of his life.

Lamar had become a Christian at an early age but like many teenagers he was curious about sex and began experimenting in early adolescence. Sexual encounters became a way of life. Lamar never knew his dad, but his concept of manhood was a guy who could prove himself on the athletic field and with women. Lamar's locker room boasting about sexual conquests plus his stellar performance on the football field made him the envy of many guys. He enjoyed the respect he got from being known as a player in every sense of the word. Lamar was courted by college football recruiters and landed an athletic scholarship. Academic pressure plus being away from home and all that was familiar made for a stressful life but the football team was like a family. When they weren't playing a game or in practice, they bonded by partying. Being a football player gave him campus-wide exposure and easy access to women. Football, parties, women and classes filled his days.

At the beginning of his sophomore year, Lamar was invited by Reggie to join a Bible study with other athletes. The small group discussions gave him a place to voice his questions. He was surprised at the thoughtful answers given by group members. The small group felt like a brotherhood. Through the Bible study with fellow athletes, he was exposed to a different kind of masculine strength.

Lamar felt like he had two lives: his party life and his Bible study life. Some days, it was hard to juggle the two identities. One Saturday night Lamar was invited to go out with his party friends. After partying all night, Lamar woke up and found himself in bed with a complete stranger. As he lay next to this sleeping woman, trying to reconstruct the events of the previous night, it dawned on him that it was Sunday morning. Immediately he thought of his mom, wearing one of her fancy hats, and the choir singing, and then he thought about Reggie and the guys in his Bible study. He realized he was the prodigal son, and he wanted to find his way home.

The story of the prodigal son (Luke 15:11-32) is about a man who left home and squandered the family money on wild living. But when he had nothing left, he came to his senses. He decided to go back home to his father. The father saw the son at a distance, ran to meet him, threw his arms around him and gave him a kiss. He welcomed him with open arms and threw a party for him.

That Sunday morning was a turning point for Lamar. He knew he could not live a double life any longer. He contacted Reggie and began meeting with him one on one. Having a mentoring relationship with a man a few years older than him was helpful in reconstructing his life. Lamar had some moments of failure. When he went back to his old life, a sense of despair would creep in. He explained with a slow smile, "Now that I have God in my life, I can't seem to enjoy sin anymore."

If you're a prodigal, feel the arms of your heavenly father welcoming you back home. See yourself being held in God's embrace. Drink in his lavish love for you. His forgiveness is real. You can pray a simple prayer like this: "God, you know I've wandered far away from you. I've done some things that I knew were wrong. Thank you for your death on the cross that paid for my sins. Forgive me. Wash me and help me get back on track to live for you. Help me to follow you day by day and seek your plans for my life. Amen."

Just like the new believer in Christ, you need a faith community to encourage you. Seek out Christian friends to help you have a fun social life that is honoring to God.

LIVING A NEW LIFE

Coming to God with the junk in our lives involves forgiveness, but it also involves repentance—turning away from sin and choosing a new life of purity. When my husband, Bill, was in graduate school, he wandered into a campus church after an all-night drinking binge. He met with the pastor for several weeks, peppering him with questions. Eventually he became a Christian and sought the forgiveness of God.

When Bill became a Christian, he knew that he needed to change many aspects of his lifestyle. He had been sexually active since his teenage years and had sexual relationships with numerous partners.

Turning away from his former fraternity practices wasn't easy. But from the time of his conversion until our wedding day, he refrained from sexual intercourse. And although he has struggled with lust from time to time, he has been a faithful husband to me for thirty-plus years. Bill is living proof that a person with a sexual past can be faithful in marriage and be used by God in significant ways. He's currently the pastor of the same church he wandered into after the all-night drinking binge. As he serves communion to his congregation, offering people the bread and wine of forgiveness, it's not an exercise in head-knowledge theology. He knows firsthand the rich forgiveness of Jesus Christ that was purchased for him at the cross.

EXPERIENCING GRACE

When I first learned of Bill's sexual past, it was extremely upsetting to me. I was waiting until marriage to have sex, so his intimacy with other women made me jealous. I felt that he had given to them what should have been saved and given to me. I also feared that I would be compared to women he had been with previously.

When I tried to process my upset feelings, I kept coming back to the fact that God had forgiven Bill, Christ died to pay for Bill's sins, and God had washed him clean. I had no right to withhold forgiveness. Also, even though I had never had sexual intercourse, I wasn't completely innocent. Even my relatively minor involvement was less than God's perfect standards. Bill and I both needed God's forgiveness in the area of sexuality.

As I took this to God in prayer, God enabled me to extend forgiveness to Bill. I realized that Bill was a new creation in Christ. My forgiveness of him and my belief that he was a new creation in Christ had a powerful effect in Bill's life. Bill has often told me that my forgiveness of him played a key role in his healing process. Sometimes it has been challenging to maintain an attitude of forgiveness and not dredge up his past or pester him for details, but I remind myself that these are memories I want him to forget, not remember.

RESTITUTION

Turning to God with our brokenness involves forgiveness and repentance, but it may also involve restitution. Restitution means taking responsibility for our sin and doing anything within our power to make things right. This may mean going back and apologizing to someone you violated through date rape. It may mean taking responsibility for an unplanned pregnancy. It may mean confessing to someone that you cheated on them and asking for forgiveness. It may mean confessing a lie. It may mean returning something you have stolen.

For Min, restitution came at an unusual time. A few weeks before his wedding day, Min and his fiancée met with my husband and me. Min was visibly uncomfortable, repeatedly shifting his position in the office chair. He was stumbling around with his words trying to get something out. Bill and I sat there bewildered. Min's fiancée seemed to know, but she kept silent, her eyes fixed on the carpet.

Finally Min put words to his troubling thoughts. "As I think about my wedding day and being able to fully enjoy the physical aspect of marriage, I, um, I have some memories that are haunting me. Um, well, when I was in middle school, I sexually abused my younger sister a few times. She and I have never talked about it. I don't even know if she remembers it. I don't know if I should apologize to her. Maybe she doesn't remember it. Also, I don't want to drop this bomb on her only weeks before the wedding when all the relatives are coming into town and we're supposed to be celebrating."

For a moment we all sat in silence. My husband broke the awkward quietness and commended Min for his courageous honesty. His desire to face his shameful past and make things right was noble. As we talked further, Min decided that he would talk with his sister. He would confess his wrongdoing and ask for her forgiveness. We prayed for Min to find the right words, for God to go before him and prepare his sister to have this difficult conversation and for both of them to experience healing.

The conversation took place only days later. Min's sister was initially surprised and silent. But as they talked further she said she did remember the incidents and had struggled with feeling dirty, wondering what was wrong with her and sometimes being angry at Min. Min took full responsibility for the offense and asked for her forgiveness. They both cried. Their conversation ended up being a healing time for them individually but also for them as brother and sister. An awareness of God's forgiveness along with clarity and freedom come when we bring the dark things of our life into the light of Christ. Min was able to enter into the joy of a sexual relationship in marriage without any cloud of shame. Min's sister was able to start working on the healing she desperately needed.

Are there some action steps you need to take to bring about restitution? It may be the hardest thing you'll ever do, but it will set you free. Shackles fall off as we own up to sin and make things right. Confession, repentance and restitution are foundational practices in the Christian life, not only for sexual sins but for all the other sins we commit.

As God begins to form you into the person he intended you to become, you should know that you'll face opposition. Satan, who is called the accuser in the Bible, will dredge up old sins and throw them in your face. "You can't lead a Bible study! I know what you did. What are *you* doing in church? A person like you has no business here. You're too dirty." When Satan throws a dart of condemnation at you or memories come up from your past sin, turn to Jesus in prayer: "Thank you, Jesus, that you died for all my sins. Thank you that I'm washed clean and that you have given your righteousness to me. I'm a new person in Christ."

Music is a powerful way to purify our minds. Consider loading your iPod with Christian music that you can listen to while you commute, work out or relax. Listening to sacred music isn't a quick fix for all of our brokenness, but many people say that music connects to a place deep within their souls. David, a shepherd boy, was brought in to King Saul to play the harp when Saul was tormented by troubling thoughts. David's music brought relief to Saul (1 Samuel 16:14-23).

Karli is still in college and still single. Her questions have not all been answered, and her issues are not all resolved. But day by day, she's allowing God to enter into the mess of her life.

Mike Yaconelli writes in his book *Messy Spirituality*:

Spirituality is not a formula; it is not a test. It is a relationship. Spirituality is not about competence; it is about intimacy. Spirituality is not about perfection; it is about connection. The way of the spiritual life begins where we are *now* in the mess of our lives. Accepting the reality of our broken, flawed lives is the beginning of spirituality, not because the spiritual life will remove our flaws, but because we let go of seeking perfection and instead seek God, the one who is present in the tangledness of our lives. Spirituality is not about being fixed: it is about God being present in the mess of our unfixedness.[28]

You may have messed up badly, but you're not damaged goods. God wants to be present in your mess. When you lay hold of the forgiveness of Jesus, the end result is a heart of gratitude, love and humility, traits that may end up being your greatest strengths.

PART TWO

Dating

19 Should I kiss dating goodbye?

What does the Bible say about dating? Actually the word *dating* isn't found anywhere in the Bible. In Bible times and throughout most of history, marriages were arranged. Sometimes the marital union solidified a political alliance and at other times a bride was the reward for a valiant military feat, like King Saul's offer of his daughter to anyone who could slay Goliath (1 Samuel 17:25). Sometimes marriage was used to obtain financial security. This happened in the movie, *Titanic*, when Rose was being forced to wed Cal.

Most often marriages were arranged between families of similar social standing for practical reasons, such as strengthening economic resources. There was always hope for love and romance, but these were secondary concerns. It wasn't until the 1800s in the United States that marriage expectations changed. Love and romance became more important. The advent of moving pictures, presenting love and romance on the big screen, stirred a hunger for romance in the heart of the ordinary person.

In those days, a young man called on a woman at her home, so love relationships began to grow under the watchful eye of the girl's parents. Courting happened in the parlor or living room. Mom was around the corner listening in from the kitchen; Dad was hovering around and little brother was delighted to have an audience to perform his latest tricks. Parents continued to influence the courting process, but the young couple had increasing power to determine the course of their love life.

The advent of automobiles brought about another radical change in the landscape of mate selection. "Coming to call" was replaced with "going out." To date someone meant going someplace. Parental consent and control still existed but more from behind the scene. A car signaled autonomy. Social contacts happened at restaurants, movies and night clubs. The mobility and privacy of the automobile also meant the possibility of *parking,* so sexual involvement increased. The 1960s marked another social change as people embraced the mantra "make love, not war." Sexual promiscuity dramatically increased. People no longer parked; they simply visited the bedroom. It was an era of liberation: women's liberation, equal rights for African Americans, the end of the military draft and sexual freedom.

The 1990s marked another major social change as technology increasingly shaped romantic relationships. Cell phones, instant messaging and texting made it possible to have frequent communication with someone—without your family or roommates ever knowing. All this one-to-one communication in isolation can create a feeling of intimacy that's intense. Personal sharing often happens in this impersonal way.

Websites and Internet sites gave singles another way to pursue love relationships. Checking Facebook to see if that girl in psych class is still listed as single can be a daily preoccupation. Discovering a boyfriend has posted pictures of himself shirtless with someone else can ignite jealousy and result in hours of instant messaging to sort it all out.

Today, meeting people has become increasingly difficult. Years ago, people walking to and from class on campus would stop and greet one another. When they stopped to chat, often they met a new person who was with their friends. Sometimes they met someone on a bus that frequented the same route. Now people are plugged into iPods or talking on cell phones, totally disconnected from people around them.

In reaction to all these cultural changes, many Christians have called into question the whole process of dating as we have come to know it. Certain Christian colleges and church denominations have had long-standing policies that forbid dating, but the idea of not dating became popular with the broader Christian community with the advent of Joshua Harris's book *I Kissed Dating Goodbye*.[1] Even though Joshua was only twenty-one when he wrote the book, he put a floodlight on many of the flaws inherent in the dating process.

The opening scenario of a wedding with past lovers joining the prenuptial couple at the altar vividly portrays the damage of uniting, bonding and breaking up with multiple partners. Harris also unmasks the rampant sexual sin often involved in dating relationships and highlights the role of Christian community in finding suitable marriage partners.[2]

Over the years, I've observed that people who read *I Kissed Dating Goodbye* and decide not to date find it fairly easy to live out their conviction to not date because it's a self-imposed choice. In contrast, people who have the no-dating rule imposed on them, by parents or religious leaders, often resort to sneaking around.

Samantha was forbidden by her parents to date, so she used deceptive means to connect with her boyfriend. She had her mom drop her off at the library front door. She got out of the car with her backpack slung over her shoulder, walked into the library and then walked out the back door where her boyfriend was waiting to pick her up. Perhaps the greater evil wasn't time with the boy, but the deception of her parents. Her efforts were directed at appearance management—looking good on the outside. Rather than being concerned with what's going on in her relationship with God, she spent her efforts on external conformity and looking good in the eyes of people in her faith community. She continued this pattern for over a year. She grew up with a shroud of shame and guilt regarding male-female relationships. Years later, she still hasn't developed an authentic faith.

I know a young man who climbed out of his bedroom window to meet his girlfriend because his parents wouldn't let him date. He found himself living a double life. He was one person at his Christian school and another person with his girlfriend. If you're in a faith community that forbids dating and are secretly meeting someone, I encourage you to talk with your parents or religious leader about it. Perhaps you can come to terms with rules you can both live with. Developing patterns of deceit and lying are probably more harmful to you than dating.

BIBLICAL WAYS OF SPOUSE HUNTING

People often say, "I want to find a marriage partner in a way that's biblical." Let's look at accounts in Scripture that describe how people gained marriage partners. Genesis 24 describes the account of Abraham dispatching his servant to go to his relatives in another country to find a wife for his son, Isaac. This historical account is a lovely narrative about faith, loyalty, love and dependence on God; however, seeking to reenact a historical narrative in Scripture is loaded with problems.

This becomes apparent when you consider the way the men of the tribe of Benjamin found their marriage partners. They went to an annual festival in Shiloh and hid in the vineyards. When the girls of Shiloh came out to dance, the men rushed from the vineyards, each man catching and carrying off one to be his wife (Judges 21:15-23). This text rarely makes it into Sunday school curricula, for obvious reasons.

Although reenacting historical narratives to find spouses wouldn't work well in our society, the Bible does have a great deal for us to consider as we seek to find a marriage partner. The Bible's clear teaching is that our first and primary calling in life is to be a devoted follower of Jesus Christ. We are called as Christians to be holy as God is holy. We are called to love one another and build each other up. We are called to sexual purity. We are called to live out our faith in the community of believers and make decisions with the kingdom of God in mind.

GUIDELINES FOR DATING RELATIONSHIPS

To help you, here are some guidelines for dating relationships.

- God should be your first love. Find your primary intimacy with God. Let him occupy the central place in your heart. All other human relationships are second to your sacred romance with God. Never try to put a person in that God-shaped vacuum in your heart. Make sure you're growing in your love relationship with God before you seek a marriage partner.

- Give your love life to God. Remember you're primarily seeking God's will for your life. That may involve marriage or it may not. Lay the desires of your heart before him and ask him to mold and shape them in accordance with his will for you. Seek to follow where he leads you.

- Learn what kind of person you connect with best. What are your must-haves and what are your deal-breakers? One essential should be that you marry a growing Christian. Second Corinthians 6:14 says, "Do not be yoked together with unbelievers."

- Invite outside guidance and feedback on your relationship. There are four groups of people who can provide you with valuable insight and guidance.

  •*Parents.* Depending on how healthy your relationship with your parents is, your parents may be helpful sources of wisdom. They have years of wisdom and marriage experience—either a successful marriage or a failed marriage that has taught them life lessons. Even if they're not believers, invite their feedback and take their advice to the Lord in prayer.

• *Your siblings.* Your sisters and brothers know you as well or better than your parents, and they're your same generation. Often siblings know stuff that even parents don't know.[3] Inviting your siblings' feedback will unearth some things for you to think about.

• *Pastors, church leaders or campus ministry staff.* Dating couples and married people need the nurture of a faith community. Seek out advice from your pastor, church elders or other godly Christians who know you and have years of wisdom. Allow them to assist you in finding God's choice. Make sure you and the person you're dating become known to your faith community.

• *Your friends.* Ask your friends if your love relationship is good for you. Does it bring out the best in you? What challenges might you encounter if you married? Your friends know another side of you. Your roommate probably knows more about the day-to-day happenings in your relationship than your pastor or your parents.

It's unreasonable to think that two twentysomethings or even two thirtysomethings can make such a monumental decision in a vacuum. When hormones are raging and love is in the air, it's easy to be deceived. Seek input from wise people who know you and love you. In an ideal world, all of the people mentioned above would give you their blessing and approval. If you encounter some opposition, make sure that three of these four categories of people endorse your relationship before getting engaged.

• Make sure that you know the person well *before* getting engaged. If you're part of a faith community that practices arranged marriages or courtship, make sure you don't make any commitment until you know the person well. You can learn a great deal about a person in a group context, but much of marriage happens between just two people. You need some time alone to see how you relate as a couple. I've witnessed many unhappy marriages in which young people have gotten married without ever really knowing the other person. They trusted well-meaning and godly people for this all-important decision but later felt deeply disappointed.

Having said this, I realize that in certain cultures, such as east Indian and Pakistani families, matchmaking is still practiced with specific ethnic expectations in place. The challenge will be to honor cultural practices and to work within that framework to get to know the potential marriage partner.

- Commit yourself to sexual purity. Spend some time alone with God in prayer and come up with a set of boundaries. Even if you're not in a dating or courting relationship, it's important to have clearly known boundaries.

- Be cautious about giving your heart away. Most Christians are aware of the danger of sexual fornication, but unaware of the danger of emotional fornication. "You can't put a condom on your heart" became a popular expression in the 1990s. Emotional intimacy can come too quickly by sharing deep things of the soul and past sexual experiences. Late-night talks that last several hours sometimes result in intimacy that has no basis. Make sure that expectations and assumptions are clearly laid out before you open your heart to another person. Have a DTR (define the relationship) or a CYI (clarify your intentions) talk before you open your heart.

- Resolve that your life and interaction will bless anyone you date. People leave fingerprints on the lives of those they interact with. Make certain that you leave a touch of blessing—not damage. If you're a person of honesty, integrity and sexual purity, you can show someone of the opposite sex what a healthy relationship looks like. Even if you don't end up together, your time of interaction will give that person a taste of a healthy relationship.

- Resist the temptation to seek supernatural guidance in the decision to become engaged. In an effort to find God's will, many people have trusted in signs instead of good judgment and confirmation from parents, siblings, church leaders and friends. Finding out that your mothers have the exact same birthday is amazing, but not a sign from God that this is the person you should marry.

- Pray. Spend time each day asking God to guide your relationships. Ask God to give you green lights if this is the one and red lights if it isn't. Ask him to help you make choices that are honoring to him.

Following these guidelines will help the light of Christ to shine brightly through your relationship. By dating in a godly way, you can also share your faith with others.

When I was engaged, I was living in a sorority with fifty-six other women. Repeatedly I was asked by sorority sisters why I did not spend the night with my fiancé, Bill. In the mayhem of fifty-plus university coeds, they were watching me so closely, they noticed whether I came home. I had more opportunities to share my faith from that one small choice than anything else during the two years I lived in the house. That one choice sparked spiritual conversations with people who never would have come to Bible study or church.

However you date, decide today that you'll be Exhibit A of a single person seeking the love of your life in a way that brings honor to God.

20 What does it take for a relationship to last a lifetime?

Several years ago, my husband, Bill, and I visited an elderly woman who was dying of cancer. As we rang the doorbell, I wondered what in the world we would say. We walked into the house, and we saw her in great pain, terribly bloated and bald from chemotherapy. By her side was her loving husband of more than fifty years. He had been the one who had fed her, bathed her and cared for her.

I looked at her in this pitiful state and wondered what she looked like on her wedding day. I bet she was absolutely beautiful. I don't remember anything that was said that day, but I will always remember the loving care and commitment of her husband, which continued through the last day of her life.

As I left their home and drove back to mine, I happened to drive through campus, where I saw a number of couples holding hands, some in romantic embraces. With every fiber in my body, I wanted to run up to them and say to the guy, "Will you love her forever? Would you be there for her if she were dying of cancer and her hair had fallen out?" And to the woman I wanted to say, "What about you? Will you love him forever? Would you be there for him if he were feeble and frail, too weak to lift his head off the pillow?" But of course they would say to me, "Whoa, lady! Chill out. What's your problem?"

As I continued driving, I began to wonder why some relationships start off so full of love and passion but then fizzle out. And why do other relationships continue to flourish and last for a lifetime?

Many people have asked my husband and me how we have stayed married for thirty-plus years. I would be dishonest with you if I didn't share the unseen force that has held us together: God.

My husband is a pastor and has worked with over two hundred couples doing premarital counseling and weddings. Of those two hundred couples only six couples have gotten a divorce. That's roughly 3 percent, as opposed to the 50 percent divorce rate of the general public. The staying power of these marriages is not found in my husband's great premarital counseling skills but in the couples' desire to make Christ central and learn how to draw from God's spiritual resources. But you may ask how Jesus Christ makes a difference in a marriage.

You and I were created by God. The order and design that we see in the universe points back to a marvelously intelligent Creator. God created us for relationships with him and with other people. God hard-wired us for love relationships.

THE MANY FACES OF LOVE

We use the word *love* in many different ways. We say,

- I love those shoes!
- I love pepperoni pizza!
- I love my grandmother!
- I love my husband!
- I love the New York Yankees!

In the English language we have only one word to describe all those diverse feelings. Other languages are richer and have more words to describe love.

Three Kinds of Love, by Masumi Toyotome, is helpful in sorting out these different kinds of love.

If love. As Toyotome describes them, the first one is *if* love. This is the love we are given *if* we meet certain requirements.

- I will love you if you get good grades and bring honor to the family.

- I will love you if you become successful and earn a large paycheck.
- I will love you if you cook dinner for me.

This kind of love is conditional and is offered in exchange for something the other person wants. It's unsatisfying because it's motivated by selfishness. Its purpose is to gain something in exchange for love. Love becomes the coin that is used to barter for what's wanted.

Because love. The second kind of love is called *because* love. There's a quality or condition in a person that makes them lovable.

- I love you because you're beautiful.
- I love you because you're intelligent.
- I love you because you spend money on me and take me to fun places.
- I love you because you're funny and cheer me up when I'm down.

This kind of love is a little better than the *if* love that has to be earned; we just don't have to work so hard. We're loved for something we already possess. Also, it's flattering. What girl wouldn't want to be told, "I love you because you're so beautiful" or what guy doesn't want to be told, "I love you because you're so buff!"

However, fear and competition come creeping in the back door. We fear losing our lovable trait or being upstaged by someone who has more of the lovable quality. If your husband loves you because you're beautiful, what will happen as you age and younger and prettier women catch his eye? If your wife loves you because you're so wealthy, what will happen in times of financial reversal or if someone comes along who has more money?

A number of years ago, Bill and I were at a retreat for married couples. In our small group, each person was supposed to share why they fell in love with their spouse. This was one of those exercises designed to help you recover your initial attraction to one another. One elderly woman said, "I fell in love with Henry because of his beautiful wavy brown hair!" She looked adoringly at Henry who smiled and returned the look of love. Then I noticed that Henry was completely bald. They were obviously still much in love. I wanted to say, "Umm, the hair is gone, so what kicked in?"

In-spite-of love. I think the answer to my question is the third kind of love, *in-spite-of* love.

> It is different from the "if" kind of love in that it has no strings attached and expects nothing in return. It is different from the "because" kind of love in that it is not brought forth by some attractive quality in the person who is being loved. In this third kind of love, the person is loved "in spite of," not because of what he is. One may be the most ugly, most wretched, most debased person in the world and would still be loved when he meets this "in spite of" kind of love. He does not have to deserve it. He does not have to earn it by being good or attractive or wealthy. He is simply loved as he is, in spite of the faults or ignorances or bad habits or evil records he may have. He may seem absolutely worthless, and yet he would be loved as though he were of infinite worth.
>
> This is the kind of love for which our hearts are desperately hungry. Whether you realize it or not, this kind of love is more important to you than food or drink or clothes or home or family or wealth or success and fame."[4]

Most marriages are built on *if* love and *because* love. For a marriage to last a lifetime, it should ideally have no *if* love, some *because* love and an abundance of *in-spite-of* love.

Why is this *in-spite-of* love so rare? Where does it come from? We cannot self-generate this kind of love. It comes from God. First John 4:7 says, "Love comes from God." God has this *in-spite-of* love for you and me and everyone in the universe. God knows everything about you, everything you've ever done or said, and he still loves you completely. He'll never make some discovery about you that will snuff out his love for you.

If you look at all the religions of the world, you'll find that only Christianity talks about a God with *in-spite-of* love. All other religions teach that God will love you if you meet certain requirements or because you do certain things. The ultimate expression of God's love was when Jesus left the throne of heaven and came down to earth on a rescue mission to die on the cross, so that we might be able to come into a relationship with a righteous and holy God. God wants to fill our hearts to overflowing with this love. Only God can satisfy our deep need for unconditional love.

God's unconditional love has an amazing corollary. God has given people the wonderful opportunity to be channels of this *in-spite-of* love. Your life can become a pipeline dispersing unconditional love to those around you. First John 4:19 says, "We love because he first loved us." When we see instances of human *in-spite-of* love, that love comes from God.

In order to have love that will last a lifetime, we need to go to God daily and ask him to fill our hearts to overflowing with his love, and we also need to ask him to give us *in-spite-of* love for the people he has put in our lives, especially our marriage partners.

I wrote some thoughts about unconditional love between a husband and wife in my journal not too long ago.

The greatest thing any parent can give a child is an enduring and loving marriage. Even other people draw security from a lifelong bond of love and devotion. Perhaps it is the mutual love of two horribly flawed people that speaks so loudly to a watching world. It would be effortless to love a perfect person, but it takes God's unconditional *agape* [in-spite-of] love to keep on loving someone who is so terribly flawed and filled with inadequacies and annoyances. Maybe it serves as Exhibit A that a flawed person can in fact be loved.

Our society communicates to us that marriage is a private matter. What happens between a husband and wife is no one else's concern. But every marriage is intended to be a living parable that illustrates God's unconditional faithfulness and love. Perhaps that's why divorces are so shattering; it has an effect not only on the marriage partners and children, but it ripples to the whole community.

Agape love. The New Testament of the Bible was written in Greek, and the Greek language has three main words we translate into our word *love*. One is *agape*. This is the *in-spite-of* love I've been telling you about that should be a part of every marriage.

Phileo love. The second Greek word is *phileo,* which describes the love between two friends. To be married is to have a best friend for life, someone to share the ups and downs that life brings us. In a marriage, even the ordinary tasks of life—running errands, cooking dinner—are enjoyable because you're doing it with your best friend. Being married means knowing that there will always be someone there for you.

Eros love. The third Greek word for love that should characterize a great marriage is *eros*. This is the sexual love between a husband and wife. We get the word *erotic* from it.

SUSTAINING YOUR RELATIONSHIP

Being able to share the burdens and joys with someone who knows you, knows your history and will share your tomorrow is of immeasurable worth. My husband and I have a habit of asking two questions each night as we process our day. The first is, what was the highlight of your day that we can thank God for? This cultivates an attitude of thankfulness, pushes us to see the fingerprints of God in our day-to-day lives and offers an interesting window into our partner's heart. I'm often amazed at his daily highlight.

The second question is, what are you concerned about that we can take to God in prayer? This gives us permission to voice our worries to one another and gently reminds us that we are called to "cast all your anxiety on him because he cares for you" (1 Peter 5:7). After this time of sharing we pray together. Not only does this keep us connected to one another, but we are continually drawing on God's resources to live. Once a week, we have an extra long time of sharing and get down on our knees and pray for an extended time. We thank God for the ways he has taken care of us, we ask God for guidance in our decisions and we seek his help for our own concerns.

Confession, repentance and forgiveness must be part of married life if it's to last. Two imperfect people will fail each other at times. Marriages that grow cold often have a long scorecard of past grievances. Being able to look your partner in the eyes and say, "I'm sorry, I screwed up. Can you forgive me?" leads to forgiveness. The cross of Christ cleanses us from sin, heals our brokenness and allows us to extend forgiveness to those who have hurt us.

If a marriage is built on romantic feeling alone, it will crumble, because feelings change. Falling in love is easy and effortless, it requires no work. But staying in love involves sacrifice and a determination to forge something. A marriage that lasts a lifetime must be based on commitment. It's a covenant between a man, a woman and God. Marriage is the commitment to learn how to love an imperfect person. In

The Mystery of Marriage, Mike Mason writes,

> Love convinces a couple that they are the greatest romance that
> has ever been, that no two people have ever loved as they do,
> and that they will sacrifice absolutely anything in order to be to-
> gether. And then marriage asks them to prove it. Marriage is the
> down-to-earth dimension of romance, the translation of a ro-
> mantic blueprint into costly reality. It is the practical working
> out of people's grandest dreams and ideals and promises in the
> realm of love. It is one of God's most powerful secret weapons
> for the revolutionizing of the human heart.[5]

Some people seem to be good at attracting relationships. But it
takes an entirely different skill set to sustain a relationship. Many
people spend life moving through a series of lovers. Once the romantic love phase has worn off, they are on to the next partner.

Sometimes people ask me, "Does romantic love have to die?" My
answer is *absolutely* not. There are many things you can do over the
long haul to keep the romantic fire burning. One day when I was
working in the kitchen, my husband, Bill, came up to me and drew
me close and said in his romantic voice, "I noticed on the calendar
that there's a red heart-shaped sticker on a certain date. What do you
have planned for us that day?"

I was confused for a moment and looked at the calendar. Then I
said, "Oh *that* red sticker! The vet gave me that to put on the calendar
to remind me to give the dog her heartworm medicine." Bill was disappointed—but I made it up to him. Romantic love is an important
aspect of a marriage, but not the bedrock.

If you want to have a love that lasts a lifetime, you'll need to go to
God and ask him to give you *in-spite-of* love for your partner. Make a
conscious effort to stay emotionally connected and spiritually con-

nected through sharing and prayer. Keep throwing logs on the fire of romance. Hang on to the truth that the God who drew you together will keep you together.

21 How do I know if I should marry the person I'm dating?

Deciding to marry someone is the second biggest decision you'll ever make, second only to your decision to follow Christ. The absolute enormity of the marriage decision is staggering. You're picking the person you could spend more than fifty years with, the rest of your life. You're picking the person with whom you might parent children. You're picking the person who will have the most influence over your life. If you feel a little overwhelmed at the prospect of making this ginormous decision, you are totally in touch with reality!

Thankfully you have a Good Shepherd who will lead you. God knows you better than you know yourself. He knows the person you're dating completely. Because God knows all, you'd be crazy not to seek his help in such an important decision.

The first step to knowing if the person you're dating is the person God wants you to marry is turning to God and asking him to show you his will. Come to God with a blank sheet of paper and allow him to write your love story.

When I was in high school, I had a guidance counselor named Mr. Snadden. I needed his signature on the bottom of my class schedule to sign up for courses. He was supposed to advise me and guide me. But I went into his office, firmly knowing what I wanted. I was unreceptive to his input and just worked him over to get him to sign. I didn't want input; I wanted a rubber stamp for my plans. I'm sure I was on the list of difficult students that ultimately influenced him to retire.

Sometimes we act like that with God. We know what we want; we just have to talk God into it, right? No, we must seek God's will and be willing to obey what he shows us. We cannot come to God with an attitude of, "Show me your will, and then I'll think about whether I want to follow it." We're on the right track when we want God's will more than we want the person we're dating.

When my daughter Meredith was dating a young man named Randy, I asked her if she thought Randy might be the man she would one day marry.

She said, "Mom, it's like this," and she held out her hand, open palm up. "My hand is open to receive Randy from God, but my hand is open to allow God to take Randy away from me." I will always remember that visual demonstration of her open palm, symbolizing her open heart. Her fist wasn't clenched around Randy. She was ready to receive what God had for her, but she was also ready to release what God did not have for her.

Meredith and Randy eventually did marry, and I have often shared that brief conversation with people who are seeking God's will for marriage. Envision yourself with an open palm facing heavenward, ready to receive, but also ready to release.

Seek God's will for your love life through prayer. Affirm your desire to know his will and to follow it. Ask him to guide you in this all-important decision. "Trust in the LORD with all your heart and lean not on your own understanding; in all your ways submit to him, and he will make your paths straight" (Proverbs 3:5-6).

Ask God to give you red lights if you and the person you're dating would not be good marriage partners. Ask him to make you aware of problems or incompatibilities that would stop you from making a decision with huge consequences. Ask God to give you green lights if he's leading you two together and wants you to move ahead toward marriage.

KEY QUESTIONS FOR COUPLES

Here are some questions to ask yourself:

- Do you share the same faith and the same level of commitment to that faith? Can you worship together at the same church? How you spend your money, where you turn in crisis and a myriad of other life choices grow out of your faith. Make sure you're on the same page spiritually. Second Corinthians 6:14 leads us to understand that a believer shouldn't marry an unbeliever. We should never seek guidance in an area that God has clearly spoken to us about in the Bible. If you're a Christian and the person you're dating is a non-Christian, God has already given you your answer. You are not to marry someone who doesn't share your Christian faith.

  Sometimes it's hard to measure spiritual maturity. One person has more consistent quiet times and a deeper prayer life; the other person has a greater heart for social justice and helping the poor. One person seems to have a more Christlike disposition; the other has better attendance at Bible study and church. Look at the trajectory of your lives. Are you both growing closer to God and seeking to be made more like Jesus? Are you closer to God as a result of your relationship?

- Does time together energize you or drain you? After you've spent a few hours together, do you feel alive and full or do you feel depleted and empty, like you need to get away and recharge your battery?

- Has your academic work or job performance become better as a result of this relationship? The first few months of falling in love can set you off your axis and throw your life out of kilter, but in time be concerned if the relationship has become so all consuming that your schoolwork or employment is slipping. Being in a healthy relationship should bring out the best in you and also in your endeavors outside the relationship.

- Do trusted friends and family members think you're good for each other? Often people who know you well can look into your life and see things you're blind to. Get input from your parents, your pastor, your roommate, your Christian friends. If you can't turn to your parents, seek the counsel of an older couple that you admire.

- Do you feel free to be you? Are you trying to remake your personality into something you're not? If the person you're dating wants you to be quiet and compliant and you're really opinionated and outspoken, take note. You can only fake it so long, certainly not a lifetime.

- Could you live happily with the person you're dating, even if he or she never changes? Going into a marriage with the plan to rehabilitate your partner spells trouble. Everyone will have imperfections, but can you live with them?

  When my husband and I were dating, he ran late quite often. I bought him a watch which helped a little, but he still ran late. Decades later, he still runs late. I decided that his running late wasn't a deal breaker for me. My husband wishes I was less intense under pressure and when we're working through conflict, but he decided he could live with it. I live with his imperfections, and he lives with mine.

- Is your partner committed to your development as a person, professionally, spiritually and physically? Are you willing to sacrifice for his or her development? Marriage is a call to mutual sacrifice, to help one another become all you can be in Christ. Make sure this goes both ways. One-sided sacrifice isn't good.

- Have you met one another's parents and extended family? Look at these people and ponder the fact that you may be spending 50 percent of your Christmases with them. You don't marry only the person you're dating; you marry an extended family. If either of you has a difficult parent, you'll need to face that challenge together. Can you get on board with relating to a difficult relative? Do you feel supported by your partner in relating to that person?

- Are your life dreams compatible? If a guy plans to be a soybean farmer on the family farm and his girlfriend wants to live in the suburbs, their life dreams are not compatible. The number of children you hope to have, the amount of energy you want to give to your careers, the importance of money, your dedication to ministry and the geographic area you want to live in, all these preferences form a collage of your life dream.

- Can the two of you resolve conflict well? Do you listen to one another's viewpoint, try to understand and then seek a win-win solution? Every marriage will have conflict. The ability to resolve conflict well is a major factor in determining whether a marriage will last. Couples who have a lot of volatile fights and deal with conflict destructively are at risk. If you have trouble resolving conflict, get help. This is an area that can grow and change. But don't move toward marriage until you do well at resolving conflict.

- Are you able to be honest with one another? Is there something you're hiding from your partner? If you're holding back truth because you fear it may jeopardize the relationship, this is a problem.

If your partner lies to his or her roommates, parents or professors, he or she will eventually lie to you. Marriages are built on trust. It's important to create a relationship in which it's safe to be honest. Integrity means having the courage to be honest.

- Do you trust one another to be faithful when you're separated for a while? Married people often find themselves in different towns for job travel, medical needs of aging parents and so on. You need to be able to rest assured that you and your partner will stay true to one another. If one of you has been unfaithful, get some help from a pastor, campus minister or counselor to help you get to the core issue and resolve it.

- Do you enjoy simple companionship like going to Target to buy shampoo and toothpaste? More time in marriage is spent in the ordinary things of life like running errands than having sex.

- Do you have some common areas of interest? The best marriages have overlapping passions: both are musical, both love sports, both love the arts, both like to work with the youth group kids and so on. These things will pull you together and build oneness. If you have no interests in common, the things you love will pull you away from the person you love.

  Having said this, you also need to allow one another to have separate areas of interest. If one loves mountain biking and the other doesn't, if one likes to paint and the other doesn't, you need to give each other space and freedom to pursue that interest.

- Do you respect and admire one another? Notice I did not say *love*. It's possible to love someone, but not respect that person. Mutual respect is absolutely necessary for a healthy marriage.

- Does the person you're dating have good friends of the same sex? Married men need deep friendships with men. Married women need deep friendships with women. A guy who only has female friends or a girl who only has male friends may be relying too much on sexual chemistry to hold friendships together. This can become problematic in marriage when there is a need to reconfigure opposite-sex friendships.

- Are you able to face outward as a couple as well as inward? By that I mean are you able to welcome other people into your loving union? If you're so couple-y that people feel excluded, work on reaching out as a couple. I think of the love my husband and I have for each other as a welcoming campfire that we invite others to, sharing the warmth and fellowship.

- Are you and your partner free from substance abuse? If you're over twenty-one and drink in moderation, this may be fine. Be concerned if either of you are using alcohol to deal with life's problems or drugs to get high.

SEEKING GOD'S GUIDANCE

While I was writing this chapter, I received this e-mail:

Mindy, I've been wondering about some stuff lately and thought you would be a good person to talk to because you have been through a lot and have seen a lot as well. Most of the time I think I'm just overanalyzing, and the things I worry about no one else normally would, but anyway here goes. John and I are trying to figure out if we are the ones for each other. We are huge analyzers and sometimes I feel perfectly at ease and think we will get married and sometimes I feel blah. John told me that sometimes he gets a sort of blah feeling as well, like he just wasn't feeling a whole lot of anything, regarding his relationship with me or his job or anything in his life, basically just no excitement over anything, but I think it was most evident with me.

Maybe we're just trying to come up with reasons for why sometimes things aren't perfect, but I guess I'm just really struggling with knowing whether or not I'm supposed to be with him. I know we're both just 21 years old and have only been dating ten months, and maybe we should just not worry about any of this. But I feel so much anxiety over trying to figure out if he's the one. I'm afraid I'll screw up and miss God's will and make a mistake in marrying John. I really do love John and would love to marry him. I guess I don't know what to dismiss and what to take as a sign.

Thanks for reading all this.
Kathleen

Kathleen is typical of many people who are fretful decision makers. Some people find it hard to pick a college, a major, an apartment. Just about any decision is stressful to them. They bring that angst to the decision of marriage.

As I talked with Kathleen, it was clear that she was wholeheartedly seeking to know and obey God's will, but she was afraid she would mess up somehow and not recognize God's leading in her life. I assured her that if she's doing something wrong, God will call her on it. God has promised to guide us. Our role is to be open, receptive and obedient. God's role is to get through to us. God doesn't play hide and seek. We can trust him to give us guidance.

But guidance comes on his timetable not ours. Kathleen's prayer was, "Lord, I want to know your will. Is John the one? Please let me know by next Thursday." She never voiced the Thursday part, but it was implicitly there. She asked God to show her his will, and his apparent silence was unnerving her. God chooses the time your lives intersect, and God chooses the time to let you know what plans he has for you. Perhaps God does not want to reveal his will at this time. John and Kathleen are both twenty-one.

Maybe God wants them to spend more time developing as individuals and deepening their individual faith. If they found out today that they are to get married to one another, they might close themselves off to much that the campus has to offer and become too intense and too ingrown. Furthermore, they would shift into wedding planning mode. When couples get engaged, they often direct most of their energy to planning the wedding instead of working on the relationship and growing as individuals.

Perhaps God is calling Kathleen to live with the tension of uncertainty. She needs grace to live with the unknown. This requires huge trust in God. Some people have demanding spirits that dictate terms to God and others have passive dispositions that expect God to drop marriage partners in their laps. In this all-important decision of marriage, we work in partnership with God. It's not all God's doing (he'll bring my future mate to my doorstep) nor is it all up to us (I need to hunt someone down to marry).

Kathleen asked God to give her some sort of sign to let her know if John was the person she should marry. She thought perhaps she had gotten this sign when she went to confession in her Catholic church. The priest had said, "You're young. There are many fish in the sea. Don't get too attached to your boyfriend." Kathleen left the confessional booth wondering if this was a sign from God. I'm sure the priest was totally unaware that she planned to use his advice as *the* definitive answer on whether John was the one. Hanging such a monumental decision on any one thing is dangerous.

The late Paul Little wrote *Affirming the Will of God,* and in it he says,

Most people speak of God's will as something you have or don't have. "Have you discovered God's will for your life?" they ask each other. What they usually mean is, "Have you discovered God's blueprint for your life?" But the fact is that God seldom reveals an entire blueprint. So if you are looking for that blueprint in its entirety, you are likely to be disappointed. What God does most frequently reveal, however, is the next step in his will. . . . The will of God is far more like a scroll that unrolls every day. . . . But the fact still remains that the will of God is something to be discerned and to be lived out each day of our lives. It's not something to be grasped as a package once for all. Our call, therefore, is basically not to follow a plan or a blueprint, or to go to a place or take up a work but rather to follow the Lord Jesus Christ.[6]

The call on Kathleen's life is to follow the Lord day by day. As she seeks him, he'll show her his will one day at a time. "Your word is a lamp to my feet and a light for my path" (Psalm 119:105). God's Word, the major way he reveals his will for us, is usually not a floodlight that allows us to see into the distant future; rather it's a small lantern that shows us the next step. This bit-by-bit guidance keeps us connected to God as we seek his will daily. If we received the entire blueprint, we might just take off and follow the plan, instead of following Jesus day by day.

Kathleen believed that God would probably call her to do something in life she didn't want to do. If she desired something, she thought it must be wrong and that God wouldn't want her to have it. But what does God say about our desires? "Take delight in the LORD and he will give you the desires of your heart" (Psalm 37:4). When I first read that verse, I thought, "Oh, cool, we get whatever we want!" But now I realize that as we delight ourselves in the Lord, we give him access to our inmost being, and he begins to shape and fashion our desires in accordance with his will. Our will and his will become one as we grow in him.

The will of God has a subjective basis, proceeding from an individual's mind, unaffected by the outside world, as you pray and seek God's leading in your life. But the will of God also has an objective basis, based on external observable phenomena like the confirmations or concerns that grow out of the list of questions earlier in this chapter.[7]

If you're wondering if you should marry the person you're dating, go to God daily in prayer and seek his will for your life. Remember the Good Shepherd will lead you in this all-important decision. Be patient as he unfolds his plan for you on his timetable.

22 Is it okay to date a non-Christian if we're compatible?

Ginger was excited to tell me about the new guy in her life. They had been dating for about four months, and she was amazed at how compatible they were. They were both diligent students who worked long hours to get straight A's, yet they were able to kick back on weekends and enjoy life. They both loved foreign films, Thai food and indie rock music. Before they met, each of them had taken a cross-country bike trip, so cycling was another bonding activity. Also their personalities were complementary. Ginger was intense and highly expressive; she brought energy to the relationship. Aaron was laid back and reflective; he brought a calming influence.

The only difference that existed was in the area of their faith. Ginger was a Christian and Aaron was an atheist. Even though Aaron didn't believe in God, he was supportive of Ginger's faith. He thought it was good for her, just not good for him. He told her that if they ever married and had kids, she could take the kids to church with her. He wanted her to have the freedom to practice her faith.

Social interaction with people of different faiths is something God calls all Christians to. But socializing with someone and falling in love with someone are two different things. The Bible teaches that a Christian should not marry a non-Christian. Second Corinthians 6:14 says, "Do not be yoked together with unbelievers."

What happens when people of two different faiths marry? In order to keep the peace, they agree that each individual should be free to have their own religion. Faith becomes a private matter that should not enter into the most intimate relationship of marriage. To keep arguments from erupting, they agree to disagree.

On one level, Ginger and Aaron are compatible. They share many of the same passions in life and get along well socially. But on another level they are incompatible. Their religious convictions will take them to different places. Here's what can happen if they marry:

• Ginger may want to pray about a decision such as moving to a new town. Aaron will think prayer is harmless but not at all the way he would make a decision. Seeking God's will is a discussion they will agree not to have.

• Ginger may want to contribute financially to her church's new building addition. Aaron may think that's not the best use of their money when they need so many other things.

- Aaron may permit Ginger to take the kids to church, but eventually the kids will come of age and cast their own vote. "Mom, why do I have to go to church if Dad doesn't go? I want to stay home with him and watch TV." There's no good answer for that one. If you say church and God are important, then you're insulting Dad. No wonder many kids from religiously mixed families decide not to hold any faith convictions. They've learned that religion divides. This is especially sad because the Christian faith should unite a couple and form a common frame of reference for life.

- Even if Aaron is supportive of Ginger going to church with the kids, Ginger will walk into church and see other families together. She may see another dad toting a diaper bag and corralling a two-year-old and think, *Wow, I wish I had a husband like that!* If she gives voice to this feeling, Aaron will feel that he's being unfavorably compared to other men. Not good.

Perhaps this disparate point of view is more easily seen in a realm outside of religion. Over the years, I have been friends with many wives of coaches. Consider my two friends who are each married to a football coach.

- Wife A absolutely loves football. She spends her free time viewing high school football game tapes in search of great recruits for her husband. She plans family meals around practice and game schedules. She's the woman who actually buys—and uses—the football field chip-n-dip set. The highlight of her year is holiday bowl games when the family gets to stay in a hotel and go to an exciting game that is broadcast on TV! Wife A loves her life. She and her husband share the same passion—football!

- Wife B only tolerates football. She's irritated that her husband comes home late because a practice went long. She hates the fact that holidays are spent away from home in some random hotel. "Our family life is totally disrupted by football! A piece of brown leather is the defining factor in life!" she once said to me. Football pulls them apart.

Married couples must share the most important thing in their lives, whether it's God or football. Being a Christian isn't an elective activity, like joining the ski club. God's influence in our lives will affect the way we spend our money and our time. Every view that we have, every decision that we make, grows out of our relationships with Christ.

Often dating couples who don't share the same faith hit a dead end. The Christian will eventually say to the non-Christian, "It's important to me to marry someone who shares my same faith. God is the most important thing in my life. Because we're not on the same page spiritually I need to break up with you."

The non-Christian is usually dumbfounded. One guy said to me, "I don't know why the faith thing caused us to break up. She knew all along I wasn't a Christian. Why did she date me for eight months and then lay this on me? If my not being a Christian was a deal breaker, then why did she ever date me in the first place?"

If you're a Christian dating a non-Christian, take a look at your spiritual condition. Do you feel close to God? Are you spending time with God in prayer? Is your non-Christian dating relationship drawing you away from God and your Christian friends? There is usually a correlation between dating a non-Christian and faith being at low ebb.

If your faith is at a low point and you're dating a non-Christian, be cautious about your use of alcohol. I have observed the combination of these three factors—low point in your spiritual life, dating a non-Christian and the presence of alcohol—to be the setup for actions that later cause deep regret. I call it the deadly threesome of dating.

Dream for a moment about the life you would like to have in ten years. Imagine you're married. On Sunday morning, you and your spouse get up and one of you makes pancakes while the other one dresses the kids. You drive to church together, where you sit together and worship as a family. When a tough decision comes up, you pray about it together. You both attend a Bible study with some people at church who are seeking to live out the Christian faith. On Saturday you join others in working at a local homeless shelter. There's a unity to your lives, a purpose that grows out of your common faith. If this is possible, why settle for anything less? What does your dream look like?

If you're in a relationship with a non-Christian, would he or she be willing to investigate your faith? It's possible that you could be the person who introduces this person to a vital faith in Christ. You might want to have a conversation in which you say, "I really care for you. It's not that I want less of you, but it's that I want more for us. I have a deep desire for us to draw on the spiritual resources God has to offer. I would love to have you join me in going to church. Would you be willing to read a biography of Jesus, say the Gospel of John, and talk about it?"

In this kind of conversation you don't want to convey inadequacy (you're not good enough) but rather potential (there's so much more we could have).

Having said that, it's important to refrain from making any romantic commitment while you wait and see if the person does develop an authentic faith, one that's self-motivated and internally energized. You want to see evidence that even when you're not in the picture, that person is seeking to deepen his or her relationship with God.

When people seek to share their faith like this, there are several ways the situation can play out. In some cases, the person does in fact come into a vital faith in God and a great spiritual oneness results. This is the happy ending that we all hope for.

In other cases, months pass with no apparent spiritual growth on the part of the non-Christian. The Christian keeps hoping things will change, meanwhile feeling all the more emotionally enmeshed. Eventually things unravel. Sometimes the Christian musters up the courage to break things off and sometimes the non-Christian calls it quits. Either way, hurt results.

Another scenario is the case when there is no spiritual oneness, and the Christian just settles for a relationship where his or her faith is kept at the edges of life. This is sad, because it is so much less than God intends. This is the great danger of "missionary dating." Resolve that you won't give your heart away to someone who does not share your faith, and that you won't keep dating when there is a spiritual life void.

It is fine to have a friendship with a non-Christian, but do not commit to anyone who does not share your same faith. True compatibility grows from a joint quest to follow God, to conform your life to the guidelines of the Bible and to draw from the spiritual resources found in Christ.

23 What can we do on a date besides drink and have sex?

Corey became a Christian as a junior in college. His conversion was real and radical. Those Bible verses (Colossians 1:12-13) about being transferred from the dominion of darkness and brought into the kingdom of light, that was Corey. His first prayer was, "Lord, I know I need to do a hell of a lot of changing!" Corey's entrance into the Christian community, with all his ignorance of the expectations, could be the making of a sitcom: *Crazy Corey Meets the Church People!*

One of the questions Corey had as he began to live out his new-found faith in Christ was what to do on a date besides drink and have sex. He was so used to doing those things that he couldn't fathom having a good time without them. It can be a challenge to think of fun things to do as a couple or with a group of friends. Here are some suggestions to get your own brainstorming primed:

1. Have dinner at an Indian restaurant, or get take out, and rent a DVD of *Monsoon Wedding, Bend It Like Beckham* or *Bride and Prejudice.*

2. Take a hike at a state park.

3. Have a photo scavenger hunt. Groups of people each get a disposable or digital camera. Assign photos to shoot (group pyramid in front of Walgreen's, shaking a fireman's hand). Develop or download and print photos. Regather the group and give best-of awards.

4. Attend an astronomy lecture and then look at the stars and try to identify constellations.

5. Do a service project together. Habitat for Humanity has day-long opportunities.

6. Go to an art museum. Find out which day is free if you're short on cash. Get gelato and talk about your favorite piece of art.

7. Go ice skating and then get hot chocolate, chai or a latte.

8. Go rollerblading and then make fruit smoothies.

9. Attend a sporting event, symphony, play or dance performance. Go to a recital or school competition if you're on a tight budget. Have dessert and talk.

10. Play Frisbee and then go to someone's apartment and make your own sundaes.

11. Rake leaves for a senior citizen. Ask him or her about what being a teen was like.

12. Make homemade pizza; have lots of options for toppings.

13. Baby-sit for your pastor or campus minister so they can have a night out.

14. Work out together; make a healthy dinner.

15. Play sand volleyball. Have everyone dress according to a theme: Hawaiian, school kids, mafia.

16. Attend a lecture on campus and then go out for coffee to discuss your reaction.

17. Rent a canoe and pack a picnic lunch.

18. Read an article out loud from a current events magazine or from the InterVarsity Press series of booklets. Talk about what you agree with and what you disagree with.

19. Get gyros and watch *My Big Fat Greek Wedding*.

20. Teach a children's Sunday school class together.

21. Go surfing, skiing or apple picking, depending on which part of the country you live in.

22. Bake chocolate chip cookies together; allow plenty of dough snitching.

23. Trade off being "slave labor" for each other. One week help wash one person's car; the next week help clean out the other person's closet.

24. Do homework together.

25. Take your grandparent out for pie and ask them what life was like before computers.

26. Contact your pastor and ask what you can do to serve his or her family.

27. Go to the zoo; take photos of your favorite animals.

28. Serve dinner at a homeless shelter.

29. Go to a kid's playground at midnight and play. Jump off the swing by moonlight.

30. Play Frisbee golf.

31. Go horseback riding.

32. Buy an item of furniture that needs to be assembled and put it together.

33. Go to a water park or swimming pool.

34. Rent go-carts.

35. Attend Bible study together.

36. Take a long walk and share the highs and lows of your grade school years.

37. Play tennis.

38. Gather some friends and play board games or cards.

39. Host a potluck. Have each person bring a dish to share.

40. Plan a holiday party (Christmas, Halloween costume party).

41. Have a bonfire and make s'mores. Sing and share.

42. Go to a place that has karaoke and sing like your favorite star.

43. Watch the sunset and talk.

44. Buy a jigsaw puzzle and put it together.

45. Go to a local bookstore, pick out a book and read to each other.

Think of the activities on this list as a way to learn and grow. You'll learn more about yourself, other people and the world in which you live. You might even learn how to play tennis or how to cook. It's a chance to know and be known in the company of friends. Christians should have the most joy-filled lives. Jesus said, "I have come that they may have life, and have it to the full" (John 10:10).

24 I've been hurt before. How can I ever trust again?

Trevor was socially gifted, athletic and had a resume that was impressive. He frequently had friendship dates with women but seemed content to date around. He was reluctant to get involved in a serious dating relationship since he was moving across the country for grad school. This all made sense to me, but I realized things ran deeper when he said, "I've been hurt before in a dating relationship. How can I ever trust again?"

Anyone who has endured the trauma of a broken romance has probably asked this same question. Whether you were the one who was dumped or you were the one who initiated the breakup, it can leave you with scar tissue on your heart.

THE DEATH OF A DREAM

When you date someone and give your heart away, you build this dream in your mind. You imagine what it would be like to be married to this person. Many dating couples actually talk about this dream: about buying a ring, about a wedding, maybe where they would like to live, the number of kids they hope to have one day.

When you break up, the whole dream goes up in smoke. Disillusionment sets in like a thick London fog. What might have been, will not be. And with that comes a tremendous sadness, a grief. In the same way you need to grieve the death of a grandparent or other loved one, you need to grieve the death of the dream of life together. Another thing that makes breakups so hard is the necessary paradigm shift in your mind. Sometimes there is the gentle and benign breakup of two people that realize they are not a match, but other times there is a tumultuous breakup where ugly traits come out, and you realize that your former view of the person was way off. That sweet girl cheated on you. That guy who said he would love you forever just walked out the door. There's a psychological jolt that comes from having to redo the image of someone in your mind.

Trevor realized that his former girlfriend, Ashley, wasn't who he thought she was. When they first met, she seemed so sweet and gentle, but later her need to control him came out. She seemed to flip out with the slightest provocation, but when she cheated on him, he was utterly devastated. The Ashley he knows now bears little resemblance to the Ashley he met two years ago. Had she changed? Or had the blinders fallen off Trevor's eyes? She honestly seemed like a different person. How would he ever trust any girl again?

No wonder divorces and breakups are so painful. The breakup forces a person to go back and revaluate everything. The words "I love you and you alone" become hollow lies. That romantic evening when you both professed your undying love, all that was a sham. Even photos of the two of you together seem horribly fake. Going back and rethinking all the details with new lenses is exhausting and disillusioning.

Even if you're the one who chose the breakup, you still need to go through the grief process. You may not feel betrayed by your past lover; instead, you feel betrayed by your own heart. Self-doubt sets in. You wonder how can you ever trust your heart in the future? If you felt that God was leading you to someone and yet later you broke up, then you may also have a crisis of faith. "I thought God was leading me to this person. I guess I was wrong. What else am I wrong about? Now I don't trust my sense of God's leading in my life."

PERFORMING AN AUTOPSY

After a breakup, it's necessary to do an autopsy of the relationship. What was good and what was bad? Is there anything you can own that contributed to the failure? Is there anything that wasn't pleasing to God? What would you like to do differently in your next relationship?

Trevor realized that he and Ashley had been way too sexually involved. Although they met in a Christian fellowship, Christ wasn't the center of their relationship. He also realized they had not been honest with one another. Trevor sought God's forgiveness for his mistakes. He vowed that in his next relationship, Christ would take the central place and honesty would be foundational.

Trevor also needs to realize that because of his relationship with Ashley, he will tend to import meaning into his next dating relationship. If the next girl he dates says, "Hey, shut the window. I'm cold," his high alert button may go off, and he will think, *She's trying to control me!*

If she locks into a conversation with his fraternity brother about studying abroad in Spain, his jealousy may flare up, and he'll get a panicky feeling that she may cheat on him. The drama with Ashley may be triggered by day-to-day events, and he'll need to be careful not to bring emotional baggage into the new relationship.

Anyone who has gone through a rough breakup needs to think

through what these high alert items will be. Catch yourself when you find you're reacting not just to the new person you're dating, but to the ghost of past lovers. Don't allow yourself to import meaning from the past into the present.

If Trevor begins a new dating relationship, and it moves from casual dating to serious dating, it may be wise to share these high alert triggers with his new girlfriend, so she can be an agent of grace. She can realize that he'll need reassurance of her faithfulness. She can be aware of his hypersensitivity to feeling controlled.

REDEEMING SUFFERING

C. S. Lewis, the British author, once said, "God whispers to us in our pleasures, speaks in our conscience, but shouts in our pains; it is his megaphone to rouse a deaf world."[8]

Many times the pain of a broken romance is what prompts us to come to Christ, either in rebirth or in recommitment. Through suffering we can gain new perspective on what's important in life.

The shortest sentence in the Bible is two words: "Jesus wept" (John 11:35). At the graveside of Lazarus, Jesus entered into the grief of Mary, Lazarus's sister. Moments later Jesus would raise him from the dead, so why did Jesus cry? I think it's because he was entering into Mary's pain. Our union with Christ is so deep that when we suffer, he suffers. If your heart is breaking, know that Christ is with you in your pain.

God has the ability to heal the brokenhearted. As we cast our pain upon him and allow him access to our inner soul, he steps in with healing power. Two verses attest to this truth:

- "The LORD is close to the brokenhearted and saves those who are crushed in spirit" (Psalm 34:18).

he brokenhearted and binds up their wounds" (Psalm 147:3).

The pain you feel today won't always be with you. Time watered by God's love can bring wonderful healing.

Pain can make us bitter, but it can also make us better. Pain can grow us in sensitivity, gratitude and a tenderness that's attractive. Some people I know with beautiful inner spirits have forged these virtues through suffering. Conversely some of the most superficial and self-absorbed people I know have had a life of ease and comfort. Everything was handed to them on a silver platter.

Another aspect of healing is forgiveness, not only for our own failings but also for the people we've broken up with. When we hold on to bitterness, we allow toxic waste to settle into our hearts. Popular author Lewis B. Smedes wrote, "When we genuinely forgive, we set a prisoner free and then discover that the prisoner we set free was us."[9]

When you choose to give your love life to God and realize that he's in control of the events in your life, you can begin to see things from his perspective. God is orchestrating from on high. He'll take people out of your life and bring people into your life. The painful losses are like surgery.

When a surgeon removes something, there is a hole and a sore place in your body. You feel worse before you feel better. The only comfort you have is knowing that the pain is for your good. If God has allowed your breakup (and he has), could you view it as surgery? Perhaps God is taking something away from you that isn't his perfect best.

Just prior to my daughter Tiffany's wedding day, we sat on her bed and recalled all the boyfriends that didn't work out. We recounted the tears and the drama of broken romances. At the time of the breakups, she was utterly devastated. She had to grieve the death of the dreams. But with her wedding close at hand, she could see all those broken romances were God's loving surgeries in her life. Tiffany began to experience a second paradigm shift. A breakup recolors the romance, but marriage recolors the breakups. God was taking other guys out of her life to make a place for Will, her soon-to-be husband. The broken romances—though horrible at the time—from this vantage point were seen as good. God was shutting doors so Tiffany might find the open door.

When I was in London at the National Gallery, I heard a lecture about a painting of a rose. The woman explained that the rose is a symbol of love. It's fragrant and it's beautiful, but down the stem are thorns. She said, "We all want the fragrance and the beauty, but we must realize that love also involves pain."

Is it possible to love and not be hurt? When we love, we lay ourselves bare. C. S. Lewis captured this idea: "To love at all is to be vulnerable. Love anything, and your heart will certainly be wrung and possibly be broken. If you want to make sure of keeping it intact, you must give your heart to no one, not even to an animal. Wrap it carefully round with hobbies and little luxuries; avoid all entanglements; lock it up safe in the casket or coffin of your selfishness."[10]

You can greatly reduce your heartache by following God's guidelines and allowing God to be the Lord of your love life, but no one can guarantee it will be pain-free.

ARMOR

One of the striking things in the gospels, the biographies of Jesus, is the way Jesus was betrayed by Judas, abandoned by Peter and the other disciples, and misunderstood by his own family, yet we can't detect a trace of bitterness. Often when I've been hurt, I cry out in prayer, "Jesus, how did you remain soft, vulnerable and open to people with all the horrible things that happened to you? How did you not develop a tough exterior?" After a painful breakup, we want to put a suit of armor around our hearts. We want to shut out any further suffering. Unfortunately, armor that keeps out pain also keeps out joy.

Learning to trust again means taking off the suit of armor. It means deciding you won't be self-protective. Your breakup may have made you wiser and more cautious, but don't let that rob you of the faith to believe that life can be different in the future. Life is a series of deaths and resurrections. This is true of our love lives. A dream dies, but God births a new dream in our hearts.

Come to the cross of Christ for the forgiveness.
Come to the cross of Christ for healing.
Come to the cross of Christ for the power to forgive your ex.
Come to the cross of Christ for the power to take off your armor and trust again.

25 I'm jealous of my girlfriend's former sexual partner. How can I get over it?

Michael asked to meet with me in a little coffee shop on campus. He chose a table way in the back, so we could have a confidential conversation. As we navigated through tables and chairs with lattes in hand, I wondered what was up. I knew he was dating Sonya and absolutely adored her. She was his first love. Other than an occasional date for a high school dance, he had not gone out with anyone until Sonya.

We chatted briefly to break the ice, but then he took the plunge.

With a pained look on his face, he gave voice to his heartache. "How can I get over my jealousy of Sonya's sexual activity with her old high school boyfriend?"

Sonya had grown up in a family that sometimes went to church—Easter and Christmas, plus an occasional baptism, wedding or funeral. In her mind, God was a probation officer who she tried to steer clear of. When Sonya and her high school boyfriend became sexually active, they were careful to use protection, so she figured she was practicing safe sex like her health teacher had recommended.

After dating for about eighteen months, Sonya and her high school boyfriend broke up and went to different colleges. When Sonya moved into her sorority, she was invited to attend a Bible study. Through the witness of her sorority sisters, Sonya eventually gave her life to Christ. She began to grow in her faith. God began to reshape her desires and dating a Christian guy became an attractive idea. Enter Michael.

When Michael and Sonya met, they were both involved in a Christian fellowship on campus and attended the same church. Each of them had put Christ at the center of their individual lives so when they started dating, making Christ the center of their new dating relationship was of great importance. Because of their desire to please God, Michael and Sonya were doing a good job of keeping the physical side of their relationship under control.

FEELING RIPPED OFF

As they became more serious, Sonya felt like she should tell Michael about her past sexual experiences with her high school boyfriend. Michael had only known Sonya as a committed Christian, so he was clueless about her past life. Sonya didn't want there to be any secrets.

While Michael valued her honesty, he was also devastated. When Michael contemplated that he was a virgin and Sonya wasn't, it gave him great pain. When he thought about the fact that she had been more physical with a high school boyfriend in the past than she was with him now, that also gave him great pain. He found himself eaten up with jealousy and feeling like some guy he had never met ripped him off. He bounced between anger and jealousy.

Sonya was keenly aware of Michael's devastation. Sometimes Michael pestered her for details of her past sexual experiences. She regretted her sexual activity in high school and realized that safe sex wasn't so safe after all. She was, however, drinking in the forgiveness of Christ and didn't want to be dragged back to the old sins of her past.

Michael had repeatedly prayed for the ability to forgive Sonya and her old boyfriend, but he found himself falling back into consuming jealousy. He would replay conversations with Sonya about "him" in his mind. He even spent time dreaming up clever and cutting remarks he would love to say to her old boyfriend should he ever have the chance.

As Michael and I talked, I acknowledged his pain. What Sonya gave away to her old boyfriend should have been saved for her husband, which someday might be him. The apostle Paul touches on this feeling of being cheated in 1 Thessalonians 4. The Greek verb used in the phrase, "no one should wrong or take advantage of a brother or sister" is a marketplace verb meaning "to rip off." Premarital sex rips off the future marriage partner of the virginity that should have been brought into the marriage. Michael's feelings were right on target.

FACING OUR SELF-RIGHTEOUSNESS

Although Michael had not been involved with anyone sexually, he admitted that he was often consumed with lust and regularly visited pornographic websites. When he thought of his own sexual struggles, he began to see himself as a fellow sinner. His self-righteous attitude was unfounded. He realized that in God's eyes both he and Sonya were sexual sinners in need of forgiveness.

When it comes to forgiving your partner's sexual past, unfortunately a double standard often exists. Many people believe that men who sleep around are experienced, but women who sleep around are sluts. Women may have less of a problem forgiving the sexual past of their boyfriends or husbands. Men, on the other hand, often have a great deal of trouble forgiving the sexual past of their girlfriends or wives. This double standard fueled Michael's inability to forgive Sonya.

I encouraged Michael to stop asking Sonya for more information about activities with her old boyfriend. Every time he pressed Sonya for details, he took her back to the storehouse of old memories. He was reawakening in her mind memories that needed to be put to rest. "You want Sonya to forget the old boyfriend, not remember him," I reminded Michael. His pestering for information and details was upsetting for Sonya too. She was trying to move beyond her past, and Michael kept dragging her back.

Second Corinthians 5:17 says, "If anyone is in Christ, the new creation has come; the old has gone, the new is here." When Sonya became a Christian, she became a new creation, the old was gone. God looks at Sonya and remembers her sins no more. God has forgiven Sonya. Michael needed to see her with the eyes of God. Sonya also needs to see herself that way.

I have a little dog named Tipper, a Jack Russell terrier. She's a feisty little dog that loves to run. When I take her on a hiking trail, she sometimes comes back with a strange "treasure." Clenched tightly in her teeth is a dead animal carcass. For some unknown reason, she loves to hang on to these dog-treasures and carry them around. Tenaciously she hangs on. She doesn't want to let go. Knowing that they are germ-infested and will make her sick, I have to get tough with her. "Tipper, drop it! Let it go! Give it up!" With reluctance, she drops the dead carcass at my feet. For her good, I take it away and dispose of it.

When I choose to hang on to pain, I'm like Tipper who hangs on to an old carcass—not a person, but a wound. I dwell on my pain. I wallow in misery and lick my wounds. I watch myself bleed. But God comes to me and says, "Mindy, drop it! Let it go! Give it up!"

MAKING A CHOICE

When Michael finds himself eaten up with jealousy, he's going to have to make a conscious, volitional choice to let it go. He needs to hear the voice of God say, "Michael, drop it! Let it go! Give it up! I died on the cross to pay for that sin. I have forgiven her. You must forgive her." Sometimes we have to discipline our thinking and choose to just not go there.

If Michael can offer Sonya grace and forgiveness for her sexual past, it will be a significant milestone in their relationship. As Christians, we have the opportunity to incarnate Christ by offering forgiveness to one another. Invariably the forgiven Christian says, "You know this junk about me, and you still love me!" Ephesians 4:32 says, "Be kind and compassionate to one another, forgiving each other, just as in Christ God forgave you." The healing in Sonya's life will be made complete by being totally known by Michael and totally forgiven. To be known well with all of our junk and yet loved is to experience something supernatural. It's to feel the presence of God.

Ironically as Michael forgives Sonya and sets her free, he himself will be set free. Listen to what Psalm 103 says,

> The LORD is compassionate and gracious, slow to anger, abounding in love. He will not always accuse, nor will he harbor his anger forever; he does not treat us as our sins deserve or repay us according to our iniquities. For as high as the heavens are above the earth, so great is his love for those who fear him; as far as the east is from the west, so far has he removed our transgressions from us. (Psalm 103:8-12)

God doesn't remember our sins. He doesn't throw them back up in our face. Michael will find freedom as he models his behavior after God.

Michael ended our appointment by saying, "I hope that one day I'll marry Sonya, but only God knows what the future holds. What I do know is that I never want to be the old boyfriend who rips off some other guy. I know firsthand the pain of premarital sex."

After our appointment, Michael spent some time with God in prayer. He contemplated the cross of Christ. If God had forgiven Sonya, who was he to hold onto a grudge? He wasn't perfectly sexually pure. When he thought of all God had forgiven him of, he found it within his heart to forgive Sonya. He resolved to never again bring up Sonya's sexual history.

Michael's ability to let go of his consuming jealousy took their relationship to a deeper level. They eventually became engaged and got married. I remember their wedding day and the look of joy on their faces as they gave themselves unreservedly to one another.

26 I'm obsessed with finding a boyfriend/girlfriend. What should I do?

When God created us, he hard-wired us for love relationships. The longing to deeply connect with other people is part of what it means to be human. The desire to be in a romantic relationship is perfectly normal. Being single in a society that venerates romantic love can be difficult. But if you find yourself *obsessed* with finding a boyfriend or girlfriend, perhaps you're looking to another person to give you a feeling of wholeness. Men sometimes think, *If I just had a good looking girl on my arm, then I'd feel important.* Or women sometimes think, *If I just had a guy calling me and pursuing me, I'd feel desirable and loved.* We look to other people to fill in the gaps in our soul. But right now, you *are* a whole person, with or without a significant other.

We're created by God for relationships—with God and with people. All of us have a God-shaped vacuum that can only be filled by Jesus Christ. We have basic core needs that God alone can fill. When we try to put a husband or wife in that God-shaped vacuum or we look to our mate to fill the core needs that God alone fills, we're headed for trouble.

Think of the story of Cinderella. The story opens with a miserable young woman. She's lonely, unloved, unwanted, dressed in tattered rags and loaded down with endless chores. As the story unfolds, Prince Charming enters the scene, and her whole life is changed. At the end of the story, she's dressed in beautiful clothes, adored by a man, dancing and happy. Prince Charming is the fulfillment of everything she ever hoped for.

The problem is that some of us grew up believing that fairy tale. We feel lonely, empty and unloved, and we want someone to step into our lives and rescue us from all of our misery. We feel that if we could just meet the right person all of our unhappiness would be wiped away, all of our needs would be met.

ONLY GOD CAN

We cannot expect another person to do for us what only God can do. What are core needs that God alone can fill?

- *Forgiveness.* You and I need forgiveness. We have screwed up. We have said and done things that are wrong. Only Jesus can wash our guilty consciences and make us clean on the inside.

- *Peace.* Only God can put peace in our hearts. Left to ourselves, we're filled with anxiety and worry. We fret and fear, but God invites us to cast our anxieties on him. He alone can take all that anxiety away and replace it with a deep and abiding peace.

- *Purpose.* We all ask questions like why am I here? and what am I supposed to do with my life? Only God can let us know what our role is in this vast universe. Only God can give us purpose and connect us to our destiny.

- *Self-worth.* If we base our self-worth on our achievements, our appearance, our money or our friends, it's on shaky ground. Knowing that God made us, knows us completely and loves us gives us a rock-solid basis for self-worth.

- *Power.* Only God can enable us to be who he wants us to be. We cannot rehabilitate ourselves. He will change us from the inside out. Through the Holy Spirit, God takes up residence within us and begins to form Christ in us.

These core needs can only be met by God. If we look to another human being to fulfill them, eventually the relationship will collapse.

Imagine two nonswimmers in the middle of a deep lake. They keep grabbing at each other in hopes of being rescued, but they just drag each other down. That's what two people are like who look to one another to meet their deepest needs.

Now imagine that a lifeboat comes along—that lifeboat is Jesus Christ—and he picks them both up and puts them into the boat knowing they can't rescue themselves. That is a picture of a married relationship where people get their fundamental needs met by God alone and then come together in love.

When I was in college, I had three girlfriends who said all they wanted in life was to get married and be a wife. The rest of us wanted to change the world, travel, have a career and so on. We had all kinds of dreams! But these three girls just wanted to get married and become wives. Sadly, all three of those women are divorced today. I remember thinking, *Why are they divorced? They wanted marriage more than any of the rest of us.* I think they went into marriage expecting too much. They looked to their husbands to meet the deepest needs of their souls, but only God can do that. They bought into the Cinderella myth that a man would solve all their problems and meet all their needs. Many men do the same thing. They think a woman will fill up all their emptiness.

What I mean by having God meet our core needs is calibrating issues of dependency. Our primary dependency must be on God. Our secondary dependence should be on our marriage partner. Yet our human inclination is to flip this around and turn to people as God substitutes. We try to fill our God-shaped vacuum with people and the people-shaped vacuum with a single romantic partner when we need the larger community in the body of Christ.

No person can be there for us 24/7/365. Jobs, housework, driving the kids to soccer practice and myriad demands sap our time and energy. Even when our marriage partner is available, they're dealing with their own stuff. Our needs are overwhelming for any mere mortal. No human can love us the way our souls long to be loved. To have your primary dependence on God is having a sacred romance in which you connect with God through prayer, reading the Bible, music, being outdoors in his creation and enjoying his presence. This sacred romance with God lies outside of our five senses. It's the sixth sense, a mystical union. In *The Intimate Journey,* Joel Warne writes about weaving God into one's life in such a way that his companionship flavors every area.

What if faith meant a transforming relationship with Someone who consistently breathed life and meaning into everything he touched? What if faith was a heart to Heart relationship with Someone who knew me deeply, accepted me totally, and had the power to increasingly restore my fragmented soul? What if faith opened a doorway into the personal reality every human heart had searched for since the day it was born? That would be the sort of faith you would not want to limit, isolate or confine to out of the way areas of life. Instead, you would want that faith to overflow the few narrow streams of your heart through which it currently trickles until it floods your whole being.[11]

FIRST LOVE

If you find yourself obsessed with finding a boyfriend or girlfriend, perhaps you're expecting too much from a romantic relationship. Realize that God wants to be your first love, your sacred romance. Pursue him with all your heart. Redirect your obsession toward God, the magnificent obsession. Allow him to meet the deepest needs of your soul.

You may get married someday or you may not. But even if you do marry, God has way more in store for you than marriage. Perhaps you need to rethink your overall sense of vocation and calling in life. God has created you with a cluster of gifts, abilities and passions for a purpose. Try to spend some of your energy pursuing your larger calling in life.

Make sure you have deep and meaningful same-sex friendships. Women need other women, and men need other men. When those same-sex friendships are in place, seek friendship with a few people of the opposite sex. They will help you understand more how the other half thinks. You need meaningful friendships, people to share life with, even if you never marry. Having deep relationships will help diminish your obsession with finding a partner. It's God's intention that we do life in the context of community.

Sometimes God wants to work with us one on one, that is, as a single person. Perhaps there are some areas that need healing before you can unite your life with another person.

Single people have the opportunity to love widely and broadly. Being single affords you great freedom and great opportunity. Is there something you would love to do, such as travel or go to school for a higher degree? Look for opportunities to serve at your church or in your community. As you give yourself away to others, unselfishly serving them with no thought of any payback, you'll find yourself paradoxically fulfilled.

See your singleness as an opportunity. It's important to be patient and allow God to work in your life to develop you into the person he's created you to be. That way you won't be missing out on what God has for you here and now.

I was working at Trinity Evangelical Divinity School in the student services office when I met Chad. He was working on a master of divinity degree, hoping to one day become a pastor. He came to my office to chat and mentioned that he had expected a seminary full of Christian people to be a lot friendlier than it was. "People seem to ignore me," he said. "People are not friendly here." He also opened up about wanting to be married, but he had never dated anyone.

I asked him a few questions and had a hunch Chad was doing what I call isolating behavior. People who exhibit this tendency enter a room, sit alone, don't talk to anyone, don't make eye contact with anyone and then exit immediately after the meeting or class. People like Chad unknowingly wear a huge sign on the outside that says keep out, yet on the inside they're wearing a teeny sign that says please reach out to me. Unfortunately, people around Chad only saw the huge outside sign.

I asked Chad if he would try a little social experiment on campus. He was game, so I said, "Starting tomorrow, I would like you to make eye contact with people, smile and say hi as you walk past people on campus." He felt he could do that. Although it seemed contrived to him at first, over a few weeks, making eye contact, smiling and saying hi became pretty natural for Chad.

After he was okay doing that, I asked him to initiate small conversations with people, anyone—the middle-aged woman working in the library, a classmate, someone in line next to him at the drugstore. Again this seemed foreign to Chad, but he gave it a shot.

A few weeks later Chad came back to me and said, "I think this campus is changing! People are getting friendlier!" We laughed as we talked about how *he* had changed.

SMILE AND SPEAK

When I was twelve years old, my family moved to Northbrook, Illinois. My dad would put a folded index card on the dinner table that read, "S and S." That stood for smile and speak. Dad instructed us to smile and speak when we had a chance to interact with someone. We were required at dinner to make a report of how we did that day with smile and speak as the new kids in town. As a prepubescent punk, I was less than excited about this family ritual. Yet I have to admit it was good training. Many years later, my kids accuse me of being overly friendly. They always tell me, "Mom, the checkout lady at the grocery store doesn't care why you're buying the cream cheese. She doesn't want to know about the new cheesecake recipe you found online." What was contrived and programmed at age twelve is now woven into the fabric of who I am.

People like Chad need to realize that a conversation is something like a Ping-Pong game. I hit the ball to you; you hit it back to me. Many conversations are dead in the water because one person takes the initiative but gets a one-word response. Good relationships have good communication, so it's important to learn to talk with people. You cannot build intimacy with another human being if you don't spend lots of time talking.

I know this can be hard for introverts. Small talk may come off as shallow and inauthentic. You may need to adjust my recommendations to your personality, but whatever your style, think of how you can connect with other people. Make sure you find some ways to connect that are authentic and natural for your personality and temperament.

INTERDEPENDENCE

Some people seem to be wearing a suit of armor over their heart. They're closed off, unavailable and guarded. They know they have needs but try to meet those needs within themselves. They're reluctant to be in interdependent relationships. If you haven't dated anyone, and have had no romantic relationships, you may want to ask yourself if you're walled off, wearing self-protective armor around your heart, or if you're reluctant to enter into interdependent relationships. If this is true of you, ask God to take that protective armor off your heart, so you can be warm, open, approachable and available in relationships.

Another factor that can prevent people from forming romantic relationships is the presence of anger and bitterness. If you've been deeply hurt in life and have been left with anger and bitterness, what you need is someone to move toward you in love and compassion. But often people react in exactly the opposite way. They move away and seek distance, fearing that they'll upset you. If you find that you're carrying around anger and bitterness, seek to be set free from these toxic emotions for your benefit and to open up the possibility of a romantic relationship.

God never intended us to lead lives of loneliness and isolation. God intended us to experience life with people. We don't learn who we are in isolation but rather in relationships. Choose to move more deeply into the Christian community in your town. Seek to develop three or four friendships with men and three or four friendships with women. You need good friends of both sexes to enjoy life to the fullest. Spend time with these friends even if they may not be potential marriage partners.

Keep your circle of close friends, but always leave room in your heart for new people. Join a Bible study or the ski club or participate in a service project. Enroll in a class, join a fitness center, do something that will put you in contact with more people. Dr. Henry Cloud, author of *How to Get a Date Worth Keeping,* recommends that you change your traffic pattern:

> People fall into routines in life: same community, same recreation clubs, same church. That's good, but it doesn't serve dating very well. . . . They may love their small group of friends, their work, or their church, and those areas of life are going very well. They would never think of abandoning them, nor should they. The problem is that this traffic pattern is not exposing them to people who are eligible to date."[12]

Many people will only go out on a date with someone they deem marriage material, but that puts a lot of pressure on the relationship. It also blocks you from meeting a lot of wonderful people as you move through life. Cloud recommends that people date to experience life, learn new things and practice relationship skills.

So many of my married friends chuckle as they say, "When I met Hillary, I never thought we would get married. She wasn't my type!" We have this idea in our head of what our type is and that can lock us up. Maybe God has someone in mind for you who isn't your type. Even if you never marry, having a rich assortment of friends certainly makes life more delightful. Cloud advises people to make the following promise: "I will no longer see dating as a place only to find a mate, but as a place to learn, grow, experience and serve other people. It's my new laboratory of learning, growth, and experience."[13]

Please let me be clear: when I recommend you expand your dating pool, I'm not talking about being sexually involved with lots of people. I'm not saying you need to marry anyone who asks you out. But do try to expand your list of acceptable people to spend Saturday afternoon with. While it's good to hold out for God's perfect person for you, make sure your heart is ever expanding and your list of acceptable people is growing.

I have heard many single people turn down social offers for unnecessary reasons. "I was invited out to dinner with a group of people from work, but I didn't go because I don't like Chinese food." Go to deepen friendships and meet new people. Go to expand your culinary tastes. Try to say yes to social offers. Cloud offers this great advice:

> Dating is a give and take. If you only see it as "taking," you're not getting it. See dating as a time to show others what being treated well looks like; then you help them see what is good in life, and you love and serve them. You never know where someone has come from—to be treated well might turn them around for good. . . . Help them to see what "good" is, and show them God's design for good relationships. All of life, including dating, should be a place where you are learning to love others better.[14]

I don't know if it's God's will for you to one day be married, but I do know that it's God's will for you to enjoy relationships with people. You have a purpose and a unique way to touch people's lives. You'll discover more of what that is as you lovingly move toward people.

28 Is it possible to be friends after breaking up?

Yes, but . . . While it's possible to be friends after breaking up, there are a few land mines you should avoid. When you have been in a romantic relationship and begun to give your heart away, breaking up is difficult. It's more difficult if it's not mutual. If one member is still trying to hang on to the relationship and the other member is trying to break free, friendship is hard to pull off.

Consider this scenario: Drew broke up with Vanessa, but Vanessa can't seem to let go. She wants to keep getting together to discuss the breakup. Drew isn't sure what more there is to say, but he complies with her wishes to get together and talk. Her request to be friends seems reasonable. He would be a real jerk to break up with her and then refuse to be friends.

But Vanessa's behavior betrays the fact that she's looking to Drew as more than a friend. She keeps tabs on what he does on the weekend and who he's with. She keeps staging reasons why they need to get together; she comes to his apartment to drop off something that belongs to him. All the while, she's hoping that their time together will rekindle the romance.

Drew is suffering from nice guy syndrome, so he can't figure out how to put limits on Vanessa without hurting her. He feels bad enough about breaking up with her and breaking her heart. How can he refuse her efforts to be friends? When Drew is nice to Vanessa, she becomes hopeful that they'll get back together.

GETTING CLOSURE

After a breakup, it's beneficial to do an autopsy of the relationship and get some understanding of why the relationship ended. This is especially true for the person who was rejected. After a breakup, people always ask the question, "What's wrong with me?" In the absence of real data, people try to read minds, and usually they're off base.

"If I were thinner, he would still be with me."

"If I were more fun at parties, she would still be dating me."

The goal of a discussion is to be helpful and redemptive. It's easier to bring closure to a relationship when you have a sense of what went wrong or how you're incompatible. Both of you should offer apologies for ways you've hurt each other. Healing is much easier when the person who has wounded you asks for your forgiveness. Don't spend time assigning blame. Seek to listen and understand. Explain your side of things, but don't spend excessive energy defending yourself. Just say, "I'm so sorry for the ways that I hurt you." After a breakup, you want to set each other free without damage. Having said this, there comes a time when you need to just move on and not keep endlessly discussing the breakup.

Drew will have to firmly but lovingly set limits with Vanessa. He will need to make clear to her that being friends is fine, but she must not use the friendship as a concealed attempt to resurrect the relationship. He may need to say, "Vanessa, we broke up. I think it will be easier for us to move on if we don't spend so much time together."

MIXED-MESSAGE SYNDROME

Another land mine to avoid is the mixed-message syndrome. Imagine that Andreas no longer wants to date Bonita, so he breaks up with her. He tells her he still wants to be friends. Andreas then continues to call Bonita every day or he IMs her late at night. Andreas wants Bonita's emotional support and female friendship while he looks for another woman to date. Bonita continues to be available to Andreas, hoping he will come back to her.

Bonita needs to realize that a breakup is a breakup. Andreas cannot have Bonita's daily emotional support and intense friendship when he isn't committed to her. Andreas is sending mixed messages. "I'm breaking up with you, but I still want to have dinner together several times a week, talk or IM each night, and have you be there for me when life comes crashing down." Bonita needs to simply be less available. She may need to say, "Andreas, we broke up. I think it will be easier for us to move on if we don't spend as much time together or talk as much." When Andreas experiences life without Bonita, he may miss her and realize that he does love her and want to get back together. If Andreas is fine living life without Bonita, it's better for her to learn that sooner rather than later.

You may need the help of a third party to clarify expectations and mediate. Having a mutual friend, pastor or campus minister involved may help keep the dialogue constructive. These people are more objective than you can be. And perhaps your former partner will be more inclined to listen to them.

A third land mine to avoid is falling back into sexual involvement after a breakup. So often couples break up and attempt to go their separate ways, but somehow, on some night they get together and fall back into their former physical involvement. They just pick up where they left off, whether having sex or just a passionate kiss.

The next day, one or both of them say, "What was that all about?" They may feel embarrassed because they acted like lovers when really they're friends. One person may think they're getting back together, and the other person thinks it was a silly mistake. Consuming alcohol increases the likelihood of this scenario.

Resolve that you won't reconnect physically with your former boyfriend or girlfriend unless you've made a joint decision to resume your dating relationship. Talk must precede touch.

FOR FUTURE REFERENCE

Enough about land mines. Here are two positive suggestions. First, when you break up and debrief the relationship, plan a strategy for how you'll handle things when you run into each other at a party.

People can live in fear of seeing their exes unexpectedly. A knife goes through the gut, and there's panic.

Talk through a strategy for how to handle the inevitable. You may want to decide that whoever initiated the breakup will come up to the former partner and say some small thing like, "Hi, Vanessa. How are you?" Exchange a few light sentences and move on. Even a brief encounter like this breaks the ice and diminishes the weirdness. Another plan might be that the person who arrives second takes the responsibility to say hi first. What plan you use doesn't matter; just have a plan.

This will not only save you the drama of running into each other but will also set your friends at ease. They realize you broke up and are holding their breath, wondering what will transpire between you. If the two of you have a great deal of drama and tension in social situations, one of you will probably be excluded from the guest list in the future.

My second suggestion is to be protective of the feelings of any future person you date. Being friends with an old lover may feel comfortable for you but uncomfortable for the person you're dating at the time or for your spouse if you get married.

When you begin to date, the new person needs to feel safe in your love, knowing you're not carrying a torch for an old flame. Earning trust may involve redefining a friendship with a former girlfriend or boyfriend. You may need to pull back on your emotional involvement with that person.

Don't spend time alone with a former partner when you're in a dating relationship or are married. If you have broken up with someone and truly are just friends, they should be glad to meet you with your current partner. It's a red flag when your old lover doesn't want to spend time with you both. I have seen many instances where a person wanted to be nice to his or her old love and was tremendously concerned with that person's feelings, but in the process was oblivious and hurtful to the feelings of the person from the current relationship. It's better to disappoint a former partner than break trust with your current one.

It's possible to be friends after breaking up, but it's complicated.

29 Is it okay for a Christian to find a marriage partner online?

In 1997 a friend of mine met a guy on the Internet and eventually married him. They were both Christians, but they were so embarrassed by the fact that they met online that they tried hard to keep it under wraps. When asked how they met, they both skirted the issue. Just prior to her wedding she asked me what she should do. She didn't want to lie, but she didn't want to let anyone know that they met on the Internet. Somehow, meeting online seemed shady.

Fast forward. In the fall of 2006, at my home church, a pastor in his seventies shared from the pulpit how he had met his new wife, also a senior citizen, via the Internet. Both of them had lost their spouses—one to cancer and the other through a brain tumor—and after years of being single, God drew them together online. With all the sparkle of two college kids in love, these AARP members shared their story. What was once considered sketchy has become widespread.

A few of the most common websites for Christians to meet potential mates are <www.eharmony.com>, <www.wherechristiansmeet .com> and <www.catholicmingle.com>.

Think of all we do online: pay bills; Christmas shop; book hotels and rental cars; get to know people through Facebook and MySpace; get driving directions; find jobs, roommates and churches; download music—and the list goes on and on. So many things have shifted to being done online. This major cultural shift has also affected dating and marriage.

The advantage of using the Internet to find a marriage partner is the fact that the Internet puts you in touch with thousands of people. Your pool of potential individuals to date or marry is so much greater with the help of cyberspace. It also saves time in that you don't spend months dating someone only to find out that there is something about them that's a deal breaker for you. For example, if a man doesn't want to have children someday, and the woman wants to have three kids, an Internet website might pick that up, but in a dating relationship you could spend months hanging out and never unearth that difference.

DRAWBACKS

There are, however, some drawbacks. Information online is self-reported. That opens the door wide for deception. Many people knowingly falsify their information feeling they will be more desirable if the truth is twisted. A man reports that he's a medical doctor when in reality he's a lab technician. A single woman reports that she has no kids and has never been married, when the truth is she's divorced and has three kids. Then there is the unintentional deception, such as the stingy person who claims to be extremely generous. We all have blind spots. Self-reporting is potentially inaccurate.

If you pursue a relationship via the Internet, be mindful of the possibility that some information may not be true. One friend of mine was devastated when she discovered that the man she met on a Christian website and began dating was married but reported that he was single. She was only one person in a string of women he had deceived in this way.

The other concern I have with relationships formed through the Internet is the great trust that is placed on compatibility. When two people are matched up on a dating website and so many factors line up, it's easy to mistakenly think the relationship will be effortless. But finding your perfect match doesn't ensure a good marriage. Every marriage is a crosscultural relationship. And we are all selfish and sinful by nature. Getting married and blending two lives is like the merging of two fast-moving rivers; there is always turbulence, froth and foam as the waters converge and mingle.

Marriage, even a marriage of two compatible people, is like being given a huge blob of soft clay. You have to work to forge something out of it. The key to a lasting marriage isn't finding the right person but becoming the right person. After you utter your wedding vows, the real work begins.

IF YOU MEET

If you plan to meet in person, exercise good judgment and take safety precautions. Make sure that you choose a public location like a coffee shop, a restaurant or an airport. Having other people around is a safeguard until you know the person well. Make sure you have your own transportation home and are not dependent on the other person. It's good to have your cell phone with you in case you need to call for help. You can always excuse yourself to the bathroom and make a call if you think you need a way out.

If you meet someone online and begin to communicate through e-mail be aware of the selective nature of communication. People only answer their e-mail when it's convenient and they're in a good mood.

A twenty-five-year-old man recently moved to the hometown of a woman he's hoping to marry. I asked him how things were going with his girlfriend. He told me, "Wow, being in the same town and having day-to-day interaction is different from talking on the phone, e-mailing and texting. Frankly it's been tough."

Make sure that you get to know the person's family, friends and faith community. Seeing a person in this relational context will give you a much fuller picture of who he or she really is. Invite the person to your church, family gatherings and social outings with friends. If you find that your Internet date doesn't want you to meet his or her family, friends or people from church, beware.

My other concern about relationships that begin online is that people can do a 180 on their view of Internet relationships. They may start out trusting too much in compatibility and finding their perfect match, thinking the relationship will be easy, but later when they encounter problems blame the Internet claiming that the way they met in cyberspace is inherently flawed. Almost all married couples go through a stage when they say, "Wow, we didn't know each other when we got married." This may happen after a year or two, but it seems to be a predictable life passage. Then when people have been married about ten years, they say, "We didn't know each other before we were married, but we didn't know ourselves either."

As much as you think you know yourself and the person you're marrying on your wedding day, years later you realize how little you truly knew of your partner and how truly little you knew of yourself. All this is normal, but the cyberspace couple may mistakenly attribute this not knowing to the fact that they met online and think of bailing out.

Marriage is a wonderful source of joy, but it's also difficult. Perhaps we need to add a theology of suffering to our view of marriage. Bill and

I have been married over thirty years, and we've had numerous fights, misunderstandings and failings. We've sunk to moments of despair when, frankly, we wished there was a noble way out. Feelings of love were overshadowed by hurt, disappointment and estrangement.

But we have also experienced moments of ecstasy and joyful oneness that seem like a foretaste of heaven. In our sane moments, we see each other as God's greatest gift, a best friend, a loyal companion, a passionate lover. Bear in mind that marriage is a call to love and to serve, but also a call to suffer.

Over the last decade I have had several friends find marriage partners online. Some have formed solid marriages that are joyous and stable. Sadly a few have ended in divorce. However you find a marriage partner, online or offline, proceed with caution and prayer. Stay deeply connected to Christ and seek his will.

30 Shouldn't we live together before getting married? I don't want to make a mistake.

Grant and Heather met during college and fell deeply in love with each other. They went grocery shopping and cooked dinner together several nights a week. Heather often slept overnight at Grant's apartment. In many ways, they felt like they were married.

Heather's parents were divorced. Her mom actually was going through a second divorce when things with Grant were developing. Hearing the update of her mom's crumbling marriage to her stepdad plus keeping up a relationship with her dad was draining.

Grant's parents were legally married but emotionally divorced. His parents lived under the same roof but led separate lives and had little romance or companionship. Grant was grateful for the support they gave him in athletics and school, but his parents did not have a marriage he hoped to emulate.

Heather and Grant had seen the heartache in their parents' love lives, so they were cautious and wanted to steer clear of making the same mistakes. They spent hours talking about what was wrong with their parents' marriages and tried to develop strategies to avoid the same pitfalls.

Knowing firsthand the pain of divorce and a loveless marriage and not wanting to make a mistake, Heather and Grant thought living together was a wise choice. They could try, and if it didn't work, they could go their separate ways and save each other the heartache of divorce. They decided not to have children until they knew their relationship was on solid ground. A person would not buy a car without test-driving it, so why get married without trying it, they reasoned.

FORTY YEARS OF CHANGE

In the 1970s many social scientists had high hopes that living together just might be the solution to the soaring divorce rate. Couples could live together, and those who weren't compatible could separate without the heartache of divorce, and couples who were compatible could get married. Through natural de-selection, cohabiting people could test their relationships in the laboratory of life.

David Popenoe and Barbara Dafoe Whitehead coauthored an article entitled, "What Young Adults Need to Know about Cohabitation before Marriage," in which they write, "Living together before marriage is one of America's most significant and unexpected family trends. By 2000, the total number of unmarried couples in America was almost four and three-quarters million, up from less than half a million in 1960. . . . Over half of all first marriages are now preceded by cohabitation, compared to virtually none earlier in the century."[15]

What makes cohabitation so significant isn't only its prevalence but also its widespread acceptance. In recent representative national surveys, nearly 66 percent of high school senior boys and 61 percent of the girls indicated that they agreed or mostly agreed with the statement, "It is usually a good idea for a couple to live together before getting married in order to find out whether they get along." And three-quarters of the students stated that "a man and a woman who live together without being married" are either "experimenting with a worthwhile alternative lifestyle" or "doing their own thing and not affecting anyone else."[16] Unlike divorce or unwed childbearing, the trend toward cohabitation has inspired virtually no public comment or criticism. It's hard to believe that only thirty years ago living together for unmarried, heterosexual couples was against the law.

This radical increase in cohabitation has continued. The May 2006 Census data indicated that in 2005, 4.9 million unmarried couples of the opposite sex were living together under the same roof.[17]

Why has living together increased so radically?

- A belief that marriage is fragile. Witnessing the demise of other peoples' marriages has left many people wary of signing on. Living together tests the viability of relationships.

- Puberty begins at an earlier age, and people are getting married later in life after finishing their education and launching careers. This extended period of unfulfilled sexual needs leads many to cohabit.

- Many people distrust dating as a way of getting to know their potential spouses. They see it as a game, a way to pretend. They think living together is the only way to know the other person. Sharing a bathroom and a bedroom is a good test of compatibility.

- Many people view relationships as a private matter. They believe what happens behind closed doors is no one else's business and has no influence on the larger community.

- The social stigma of "living in sin" is almost nonexistent. Society turns a blind eye to what used to be considered scandalous.

- Renting two apartments is expensive. Marriages are expensive, and divorces are expensive. A couple who lives together (and later may separate) doesn't incur these costs.

- Many people believe that there is less emotional pain if cohabiting couples break up than if a married couple does so.

No Positive Contribution

Pamela Smock, an associate professor of sociology at the University of Michigan, has done extensive research with cohabiting couples through the Institute for Social Research. In the abstract of "Cohabitation in the United States: An Appraisal of Research Themes, Findings and Implications," she writes, "Cohabitation has risen dramatically in the United States in a very short time. So, too, has the amount of sociological research devoted to the topic. In the span of a bit more than a decade, family sociologists and demographers have produced a large and rich body of research, ranging from documentation of cohabitation to assessment of its various consequences and implications."[18]

Reviewing Smock's research, Diane Swanbrow states, "While common sense suggests that premarital cohabitation should offer couples an opportunity to learn about each other, increasing their chances for successful marriage, the evidence suggests just the opposite. . . . Premarital cohabitation tends to be associated with lower marital quality and increased risk of divorce."[19]

Every study done on cohabitation indicates that it actually increases the likelihood of divorce. Even when researchers look only at the couples who make it to the marriage altar, cohabiting couples who marry have significantly higher divorce rates and significantly lower marital satisfaction rates. Living together before marriage may seem harmless or even wise until you take a careful look at all the research. No positive contribution of cohabitation to marriage has ever been documented. In addition to the increased likelihood of divorce and the decreased marital satisfaction, check out these other findings:

- Rates of depression among cohabiting couples are more than three times what they are among married couples.[20]

- Two studies, one in Canada and the other in the United States, found that women in cohabiting relationships are about nine times more likely to be killed by their partner than women in marital relationships.[21]

- People who cohabit are much more likely to come from broken homes. Those who experienced parental divorce, fatherlessness or high levels of marital discord during childhood are more likely to form cohabiting unions than children who grew up in families with married parents who got along.[22]

Many within the research community are wondering about the consistently high association between cohabitation and divorce. The first reaction usually given is the fact that those willing to live together before marriage are more unconventional and less committed to the institution of marriage. But even when researchers control for the free spirit factor, the negative effect of cohabiting on marriage stability remains.

Couples who live together place a greater value on their own autonomy than on the longevity of the relationship. Some speculate that once this low commitment, high autonomy style of relating is established, it's hard to unlearn. Conflict resolution skills are not incorporated as well when the option to bail out is ever present. Relationships are viewed as fragile and experimental. When personal happiness and fulfillment becomes the most important criterion in evaluating any relationship, things will undoubtedly unravel.

As mentioned earlier by Grant and Heather, "A person wouldn't buy a car without test-driving it, so why get married without trying it?" When I first heard that argument, I remember saying, "Yes, but people are not cars. I trade in my car every five years. I know my husband doesn't want me to ever trade him in!"

A marriage is so much more than a piece of paper. It's also more than a social construct, a place to find personal fulfillment and happiness. Marriage is a covenant between one man, one woman and God. This sacrament is enacted in the company of family and friends, a witnessing community that upholds the marital bond. It's public, not private. "Marriage is not a joining of two worlds, but an abandoning of two worlds in order that one new one might be formed. In this sense, the call to be married bears comparison with Jesus' advice to the rich young man to sell all his possessions and to follow Him. It is a vocation to total abandonment."[23]

This radical abandonment of oneself is formalized by the wedding vows. Only after the ceremony do we realize how incredibly lofty they are. Couples spend the rest of their married years growing into their wedding vows. Vows serve as sign posts directing them in the ways of marital devotion.

My definition of marriage is this: marriage is the commitment to learn how to love an imperfect person. If the only glue that holds relationships together is a feeling of romantic love, the relationship is doomed to failure because hearts are so fickle. Feelings change like the weather. Falling in love is easy and effortless; it requires no work. But staying in love involves sacrifice, nurture and a determination to forge a strong relationship.

Sometime after the wedding, the bride and groom will undoubtedly be confronted with their own lovelessness. Marriage strips us bare, and we realize that we are utterly selfish. Our own human resources are too feeble to love for a lifetime. We must go to God, the source of love and faithfulness, to keep the fires of love burning. "Love comes from God. . . . God is love" (1 John 4:7, 16). The God who draws you together will keep you together. He will give you the resources necessary, if you open yourself to his Spirit.

Marriages that last a lifetime must be based on commitment to God and to the marriage partner. Marriage is the fundamental building block in any society. A community is only strong and healthy if it contains strong and healthy marriages.[24]

MARRIAGE AS A PICTURE

One of the astounding concepts in Scripture is the fact that the marriage relationship is used as an analogy to describe God's covenantal relationship with his people. In the Old Testament, God is said to take the nation of Israel as his people, his bride. In the New Testament, Jesus is said to be the bridegroom and the church is his bride. Is it possible that the best thing on earth to describe God's amazing love is our marriages? Every marriage is intended to tell a story to the entire community. It's a living parable showing forth God's unconditional love and faithfulness.

The clearest teaching in Scripture on marriage is found in Matthew 19:3-9. The Jewish religious leaders came to Jesus and posed a question.

Some Pharisees came to him to test him. They asked, "Is it lawful for a man to divorce his wife for any and every reason?"

"Haven't you read," he replied, "that at the beginning the Creator 'made them male and female,' and said, 'For this reason a man will leave his father and mother and be united to his wife, and the two will become one flesh'? So they are no longer two, but one. Therefore what God has joined together, let no one separate."

"Why then," they asked, "did Moses command that a man give his wife a certificate of divorce and send her away?"

Jesus replied, "Moses permitted you to divorce your wives because your hearts were hard. But it was not this way from the beginning. I tell you that anyone who divorces his wife, except for sexual immorality, and marries another woman commits adultery."

Jesus' answer takes the Pharisees back to Genesis 1:27 and 2:24, and reaffirms God's original ideal for marriage. It's God who joins two people together in marriage. The union is complementary: male and female. The union is exclusive: leaving father and mother. The union is intimate: the two will become one flesh (which refers to sexual union and soul union). The union is permanent: what God has joined together, let man not separate.

MARRIAGE IN COMMUNITY

In biblical times marriages did not function as autonomous isolated dyads—two people alone trying to figure out how to make a marriage work. Instead marriages were anchored in Israelite families, clans and tribes. One of the challenges we face today is how to offer support and encouragement to marriages. Marriages need to be anchored in the larger Christian community that can help them out when things get tough. Older couples mentoring younger couples is powerful, especially for people from broken homes. Marriage enrichment classes in which couples can assess their strengths and weaknesses and get training in conflict resolution is another idea. These classes offer information and provide a network of couples to learn from. Just knowing that other couples are wrestling with the same issues is comforting.

Grant and Heather's desire to avoid the mistakes of their parents is commendable, but if their hope is to have a lasting marriage, living together isn't the route to go. A look at the research literature on cohabitation will help them see the situation realistically. Finding an older couple with a healthy and loving marriage to mentor them is a good idea. Placing their relationship within a larger faith community gives them the support they need. With God's help they can overcome the patterns of their families and have a wonderful marriage.

31 How can I tell if we're friends or dating?

Katie was glowing. No, she was bubbly and glowing. I had never seen her so happy and animated. As she detailed all that was developing between her and Neil, I realized she had fallen in love. She told me how they had dinner together three or four or even five nights a week. They spent hours talking about classes, friends, high school, life and career plans. Neil and Katie had opened up to each other and shared their pain and their joys, their fears and their secret dreams. Phone calls, instant messages, text messages and e-mails were daily occurrences. The turning point in their relationship happened when they were watching TV in the dorm lounge and fell asleep in one another's arms. They accidentally slept all night snuggled on the couch. Katie was thrilled to be dating a wonderful guy like Neil.

With this love story as a backdrop you can imagine my surprise when I met with Neil later that week and he mentioned that he wasn't dating anyone. "Really? What about Katie?" I said.

"Oh, we're just friends," Neil said. "I love being with her. She's my best friend, but I'm still looking for that special someone." I was shocked. I hardly knew what to say. Both Katie and Neil were being completely honest with me, and yet the assessment of their relationship was as different as night and day.

This scenario is typical of the confusion that exists today. In this age of romantic uncertainty a first kiss might mean *we're dating* to one person and *I think you're wonderful* to another. Like Katie and Neil, people have different assessments of the same situation. Facebook and MySpace help a little, where people are forced to designate a category: in a relationship, single or complicated. But despite this push for clarity, many relationships exist outside cyberspace labels.

The disconnect can partially be explained by the fact that many women measure commitment by amount of time spent together, frequency of communication and relational intensity. Most men are unaware of this assessment system. Women also think that an arm around them while watching a movie says they're more than friends. For many men it means they feel close to the woman they are with. It may be a little dangerous to lay out these gender stereotypes because there are always exceptions. Women can also unintentionally lead men to believe they're more committed than they really are.

THE SPEED OF DATING

Relationships today are intense and progress at high-speed Internet rates. As recently as the mid-90s, if you wanted to call someone, you called on the home phone that was probably wired to an outlet in the kitchen. Mom was there making dinner, so when your significant other called, the conversation was less than personal. Even if you were living with roommates, you shared a home phone, so your friends knew about the budding romance. Relationships grew in the soil of community and were public domain. They unfolded over time. Communication happened at the speed of a snail. In this bygone era, relationships simmered slowly in the crock pot; now they sizzle in the microwave.

With the advent of personal cell phones, e-mail, text messages and instant messaging, it's possible to have frequent communication with someone, without your family or roommates ever knowing. All this one-to-one communication in isolation is intense. The nature of these electronics may make you feel free to share personal material you might be afraid to share in person.

As you navigate through the confusion of whether you have friendship or are dating, the place to start is to be mindful of the fact that great misunderstandings can take place. There are some male-female differences in interpretation. As simplistic as it sounds, it's probably good to have an honest conversation about where your relationship stands. The DTR (define the relationship) talk can save so much heartache and misunderstanding. The CYI (clarify your intentions) talk can clear up confusion.

Many women wish this conversation would be initiated by men. It can be frustrating for women to be pursued by men who never state their intentions. This causes women to spend hours with their girlfriends trying to decode men's behavior.

Guys, if there's a Katie in your life, talk to her. Realize that for some women daily communication, eating dinner together and touch sends the message that the two of you are more than friends.

If you're a Katie, perhaps you need to be less available. No man should be allowed to dominate your social life, have your emotional support and put his arm around you without declaring his intentions. If he doesn't initiate a conversation about your relationship, it's fair for you to initiate the DTR or CYI talks.

Neil and Katie finally had the DTR talk. Neil leveled with her that he thought of her as a best friend, but not a girlfriend. Katie was devastated. She thought she had read the signals right and was shocked. Katie was deeply disappointed, but she was also liberated to move on and allow herself to be open to a relationship with someone else.

So often in the busyness of life, we don't take time to listen to our hearts. Slowing down and taking time for introspection to uncover your intentions in a relationship is wise. Psalm 139:23 says, "Search me, God, and know my heart." David, the author of this psalm, invites God to search his heart and uncover all that is buried there. We can ask God for help with the same thing. Knowing the true intentions of your heart and being up-front with them can save you and those you hang out with a great deal of heartache.

32 What's the deal with submission and headship?

Marc and Gayle had been dating for several months. They met during a weeklong service trip to help hurricane victims and were drawn to each other's heart for social justice. Things were going so well that they wondered whether they might be the ones for each other. They had so many similarities and brought out the best in each other.

But their different church backgrounds sometimes caused conflicts. Things could erupt in a flash. It seemed like they were both standing in ankle-deep kerosene and periodically someone would accidentally drop a match and a fire would flare up. The match that ignited usually was the topic of male-female roles in marriage.

Marc was from a conservative Christian church where leaders in the church and home were men. Women were taught to be submissive. He sometimes wondered why Gayle wanted to buck the system.

Gayle, on the other hand, grew up in a Christian church where both men and women served in leadership roles. She worked as a software programmer in the corporate world where women were regarded as equal participants. Gayle bristled at Marc's attempts to get her to submit to him. They made an appointment with my husband and me to talk about their clashes.

SUBMIT TO ONE ANOTHER

We decided it would be helpful to take a look at Ephesians 5 where the apostle Paul lays out guidelines for household relationships: husband-wife, parent-child and master-slave.

Submit to one another out of reverence for Christ.

Wives, submit yourselves to your own husbands as you do to the Lord. For the husband is the head of the wife as Christ is the head of the church, his body, of which he is the Savior. Now as the church submits to Christ, so also wives should submit to their husbands in everything.

Husbands, love your wives, just as Christ loved the church and gave himself up for her to make her holy, cleansing her by the washing with water through the word, and to present her to himself as a radiant church, without stain or wrinkle or any other blemish, but holy and blameless. In this same way, husbands ought to love their wives as their own bodies. He who loves his wife loves himself. After all, people have never hated their own bodies, but they feed and care for them, just as Christ does the church—for we are members of his body. "For this reason a man will leave his father and mother and be united to his wife, and the two will become one flesh." This is a profound mystery—but I am talking about Christ and the church. However, each one of you also must love his wife as he loves himself, and the wife must respect her husband. (Ephesians 5:21-33)

The opening verse provides the overarching principle that should govern all human relationships: submit to one another out of reverence to Christ. Submission is a virtue that should characterize all Christian men and women.

Other passages in the Bible also consider submission a virtue. In James 3:17, the author says, "The wisdom that comes from heaven is first of all pure; then peace-loving, considerate, *submissive*, full of mercy and good fruit, impartial and sincere" (emphasis added). In this verse, James is talking to Christians in general, not one specific gender. He uses submissiveness to describe heavenly wisdom and godly people.

If you own several Bibles, it's an interesting exercise to compare the placement of verses 21 and 22 of Ephesians 5. Are they printed back to back or are they separated? Some Bibles have verse 21 at the end of one section, and verse 22 starting a new paragraph under a separate heading such as "Wives and Husbands." This decision to put verse 21 and 22 in the same or separate sections has been a political football that has been tossed back and forth by Bible translators through the years.

Although some Bible translators have separated verse 21 and 22, the construction of the original language strongly suggests that they not be separated. In the original manuscripts the Greek reads: "Submit to one another out of reverence for Christ. *Wives to* your husbands as to the Lord." Did you notice? *Submit* isn't in verse 22. Translators have supplied it from the preceding verse. Therefore, verses 21 and 22 must be placed back to back. To separate them is misleading. Ephesians 5:21 clearly teaches that both the husband and the wife are called to submit to one another. Mutual submission should characterize every Christian marriage. Gayle should submit to Marc if they marry, and Marc should submit to Gayle.

You may be wondering what the big deal is about separating these two verses and starting a new paragraph. The problem happens when someone preaches on Christian marriage and completely skips verse 21 and starts with verse 22. They mistakenly convey the idea that submission is one way, that only the wife submits to the husband. This half-truth is the cause of many problems in marriage. Also, it's potentially damaging for those outside the faith to think that submission is for wives only.

WHAT IS SUBMISSION?

What exactly does submission mean? What would it look like for a person to submit to his or her marriage partner? To submit to another person is to lay aside your rights for the benefit of another. It is to let go of having your own way, and consider the needs and concerns of your marriage partner as more important than your own.

One of the great problems in marriage is the tug of war that exists between two strong wills. Each person wants their own way. This may play out in overt conflicts or in smoldering silence. Marriage uncovers our stubborn selfishness.

Mike Mason describes this clashing of the wills in *The Mystery of Marriage:*

> In marriage it so happens that the Lord has devised a particu-
> larly gentle (but not less disciplined and effective) means for
> helping men and women to humble themselves, to surrender
> their errant wills. Even the closest of couples will inevitably find
> themselves engaged in a struggle of wills, for marriage is a wild,
> audacious attempt at an almost impossible degree of coopera-
> tion between two powerful centers of self-assertion. Marriage
> cannot help being a furnace of conflict, a crucible in which
> these two wills must be melted down and purified and made to
> conform. Most people do not realize that this is what they are
> signing up for when they get married, but this is what invari-
> ably faces them.[25]

Mutual submission defuses escalating conflict. It brings peace to
the battle between two wills. As people let go of their way and seek
the well being of others, harmony reigns.

Why is the wife, in particular, instructed to submit to her husband if submission is a Christian virtue for both genders? The new
instructional piece is found in the phrase, "as to the Lord." She is to
see submission to her husband as an expression of her submission
to the Lord. With the same love and devotion she submits to the
Lord, she submits to her husband. "For the husband is the head of
the wife as Christ is the head of the church, his body, of which he
is the Savior. Now as the church submits to Christ, so also wives
should submit to their husbands in everything." How does the
church submit to Christ? The submission of the church to Christ is
a voluntary, joyful and thankful response to the wonderful sacrifice
he has made by dying on the cross for our benefit. Her submission

is likewise a voluntary, joyful and thankful response to her husband.

It's important to consider the cultural context of this passage. At the time the apostle Paul penned the book of Ephesians, women held a low position in society. Biblical scholar Joachim Jeremias writes, "Women were considered the property of men. Women took no part in public life. They did not vote, did not own property, and they were confined to home."[26] Married women were under the rule of their husbands. But the inferior role of women in society took on new meaning with the proclamation of the gospel. Relationships were reordered in Christ. The apostle Paul states in Galatians 3:28, "There is neither Jew nor Gentile, neither slave nor free, neither male nor female, for you are all one in Christ Jesus."

Existing social structures were not abolished, but rather were infused with new attitudes. For example, slavery wasn't abolished, but slaves were instructed to serve their masters wholeheartedly as if they were serving the Lord. Slave owners were to realize that both the slaves' Master and their Master is in heaven, and God doesn't favor masters over slaves. While the wife's submission had been required by law, she's instructed to voluntarily submit to her husband, as a result of being filled with the Spirit and as an expression of submission to the Lord.

WHAT IS HEADSHIP?

I did my master's thesis at Trinity Evangelical Divinity School on the husband-wife relationship, comparing three popular views. My study led me to believe that headship refers to a special ministry responsibility of the husband.

The husband is said to be the head of his wife as Christ is the head of the church, his body of which he's the Savior. The term *head* is used in many ways throughout the Bible. It can mean ruler, governor, boss and source (like a showerhead or the head of a trail). With this great variety of meanings, we look to the context of Ephesians 5:21-30 to understand the meaning. What do the verses that follow direct us to understand about headship?

When the apostle Paul elaborates on what exactly this headship looks like, he uses the analogy of Christ's sacrificial love for the church. The husband is called to love his wife as Christ loved the church when he gave himself up for her. Christ's sacrificial love for the church spoken of in Ephesians 5:25-27 is purposeful. It accomplishes something significant. Christ gave himself up to make the church holy and to present the church to himself as radiant, holy and blameless. This model is set forth for husbands. Headship is expressed in radical self-giving love. He's to use all his efforts to help his wife become all she was created to be.

Many sermons have been preached stating that headship means the husband has the right to pull rank if he and his wife disagree on some issue. This represents a misunderstanding of the text. No one is given a green light to have his or her own way. God isn't the author of confusion and won't lead the husband in one direction and the wife in another. If husbands and wives disagree, they should spend more time talking to one another in an effort to understand the partner's point of view, values and concerns. Then they should get down on their knees, pray and seek God's will. Each should say, "Lord, not my will but your will be done. Show us your will." I've seen family disasters when husbands pull rank and take the family in a direction the wife does not think is God's leading.

The Ephesians text is a call for husbands to love their wives as they love their own bodies. This certainly means emotionally and spiritually feeding them as well as physically. The standard of love and nurture is nothing less than Christ's self-sacrifice for the church. Some Christians want to empty headship of all meaning and claim that there is nothing distinctive about being a husband or a wife. Although there is some room for debate about the precise meaning of headship, I do not think we can dismiss this concept.

Regardless of how you understand headship, the reality is that married people form a partnership in which they collaborate with mutual respect, value and care. While the Bible has instructed husbands and wives in different ways, both the husband and the wife should exercise leadership in the home. Their different abilities and gifts will lead them to take on different areas of responsibility. Tasks will be redistributed as life changes. A husband may take on a greater share of the housecleaning during pregnancy, and correspondingly the wife may pick up some of a husband's usual chores if he's crunched at work.

LOVE AND RESPECT

Ephesians 5:31 affirms the unity God intended for marriage, originally presented in Genesis 2:24. The passage ends with a recap of all that proceeds, "However, each one of you also must love his wife as he loves himself, and the wife must respect her husband" (Ephesians 5:33).

Over the years, I have come to believe that the core need of women is to be loved and cherished, to be actively pursued by their partners and to know the security of love that won't let her go. They long to be loved sacrificially by their husbands who expend their energy to help them become all they can be in Christ.

I have also come to believe that men's core need is for respect. They long for their wives to admire them and see them as able to impact their world and their families for good. They need to know there's a calling on their lives and that they are sufficient to the task.

From interacting with many married people over the years, I know the two biggest complaints women have about their husbands are that husbands tend to be passive and uninvolved in family life and they demand their own way.

I also know the two biggest complaints men have about their wives are that their wives don't respect them and their wives try to control them.

Interestingly, these marital problems could be solved if the concepts taught in Ephesians 5 were implemented by the power of the Holy Spirit.

Marc and Gayle began to see the beauty of God's plan for marriage. When Gayle learned that submission was mutual and not one way, her defenses melted. The idea of Marc and her laying aside their rights and seeking the other's welfare was a breath of fresh air to them.

When Marc saw that God's call for him was to sacrificially love Gayle and expend his energy to help Gayle become all she could be in Christ, he realized how his old view of rights needed to give way to a view of responsibility. Gayle was drawn into the idea of Marc taking the initiative for their spiritual development.

Marc and Gayle found that learning new ways to relate did not happen overnight, but with a desire to understand and implement the teaching of the Bible, they had a common source to shape their relationship.

33 I'm wondering if we should break up. How do I know?

Any relationship will have its ups and down, and all relationships take work, but how do you know when God is leading you to break up? What are the signs that it's just not working out and that you would both be better off to part company and go your separate ways?

Alex had been dating Mimi for about a year and a half. Over the months they had a lot of conflict, but they also had some wonderful times. Things began to unravel when Alex left town for the summer to do an internship. After a long day on the job, Alex found himself feeling resentful that he had to call Mimi and check in. Granted he wasn't a telephone person, but nights that Mimi had to work late felt like a breath of fresh air. Instead of looking forward to their talks, he was relieved when he had a night off. This served as an early warning sign that perhaps something was wrong. Being exhausted and spent from a full day can leave you wishing for some down time to decompress, but in a healthy relationship there is a deep longing to connect and process your day or spend time with the one you love.

At his internship workplace, Alex found himself withholding the fact that he had a girlfriend. He didn't want the new women he was meeting at the office to think he was taken. He wanted to be free to get to know other women. Alex knew that even married people can have attractions to people outside the marriage, but his need to be seen as single left him feeling unsettled. Keeping Mimi a secret gave him pangs of guilt, but he wondered, "Why am I feeling guilty? I'm not doing anything wrong."

When Alex returned home, his relationship with Mimi went south. Little problems from the past seemed to have grown. It was hard for the two of them to get through a weekend without a major argument. Although there wasn't one huge thing he could point to, Alex began to wonder if they had the stuff to hold a relationship together.

He spent some time in prayer seeking God's will. The last thing he wanted to do was hurt Mimi, but he didn't want to stay in the relationship out of duty or obligation. For several days Alex couldn't eat or sleep. Alex wondered how he could know whether he and Mimi should break up.

RED FLAGS

Here are some red flags that might indicate a couple needs to break up:

- You and the person you're dating are not on the same page spiritually. When you began dating he or she seemed so interested in spiritual things, but the desire to pursue God seems to have faded. You find yourself prodding your partner to attend church, Bible study or Christian events. The oneness you hoped to have spiritually hasn't materialized.

- Your partner cheated on you or demonstrated other dishonest behavior, such as lying, shoplifting, cheating on a test or destroying a parking ticket, claiming they never saw it.

- Sometimes your partner is abusive—physically, sexually or verbally.

- You don't trust one another. You fear that your partner might cheat on you, drink too much or steal something if you're not there to monitor things.

- Trusted friends, parents, family and siblings are not supportive of your relationship. When you check in with key people in your life, they express major reservations.

- Time together is draining rather than energizing.

- You find your worst traits are brought out by the person you're dating. For example, your temper flares or you're critical of others when you spend time together.

- You seem to get embroiled in constant conflicts. You can't make it through a weekend without an argument erupting.

- Deep inside you wish you could date other people or meet someone new.

- You feel reluctant to introduce the person you're dating to family and friends.

- You keep trying to make yourself into someone you're not in order to please your partner. You don't think that you, as you are, are good enough.

- The family of the person you're dating is intolerable. You find yourself making excuses to avoid attending social events with your partner's family.

- You find it hard to be honest. You know you're withholding significant information.

- You seem to have different life goals and dreams. For example, it could spell trouble if your significant other wants to live modestly in the country and you're drawn to fast-paced urban life.

- You don't seem to be a priority in your partner's life. You feel neglected. The demands of a job, other friends and hobbies seem to come before you.

- Your partner's drinking habits concern you. You don't like the person they become when consuming alcohol.

- Your partner uses drugs.

- You're just not a match. Somehow you don't seem compatible.

A number of these red flags appeared in Alex's relationship with Mimi. Time together was draining. They seemed to bring out the worst in each other and others. As the weeks rolled on, Alex began to get some clarity on his relationship with Mimi. It was rather disconcerting for Alex to realize that he loved Mimi so passionately a few months ago yet now found himself fabricating excuses to avoid spending time with her. Alex knew it would be hard to deal with her tears and emotions. He felt he had to be honest and finally broke up with her. After weeks of ambivalence, Alex felt relieved to have come to a decision and broken off the relationship, but he also felt deeply alone.

Sometimes these red flags appear, and couples like Alex and Mimi realize that they should break up. But in other cases, couples don't break up but realize that they need to change and grow. Often in the crucible of relationships, our imperfections come to the surface. People can learn conflict resolution skills, and people can change their drinking habits if they realize how adversely others are affected when they drink too much. The hopelessly sloppy person can learn to be neater, and the neat person can learn to extend grace. Healthy relationships learn to work through differences in personality styles and to temper one another's extremes.

As a couple, how motivated are you to work on your junk? Are you willing to get help if you need it?

CHANGING THE DYNAMICS

Harish and Yvette met at work and began dating. When problems arose in their relationship they wondered if they should call it quits. Harish was devoted to his job and found it hard to break away from work at the end of the day. Weekends were often spent getting caught up on work. Initially, Yvette was drawn to Harish's excellence at the office, but later she began to feel like he was a workaholic. Sometimes Harish smoked weed to deal with all the stress he felt.

All this left Yvette upset, but she found it hard to be honest with Harish. Her family motto, just be nice, made it hard for her to express her true feelings. Often she withdrew into her shell. Harish could never figure out what triggered her stone-cold silence and was frustrated by her moodiness. For months they seemed stuck in this dance. The same scenario played out week after week.

The catalyst for change came from Yvette's roommate. She coached Yvette to be more honest with Harish. Speaking the truth in love (Ephesians 4:15) became the basis for a new way of relating. Yvette's roommate likened the three parts of communication (speak, truth, love) to a three-legged stool. If you remove any leg, the stool collapses. If a person speaks truth without love, it's brutal. If a person speaks love without truth, it's deceptive flattery. If a person loves and is truthful but never speaks, feelings of affection remain a secret.

Yvette's newfound honesty transformed the dynamics in their relationship. Honesty begets honesty. As their communication deepened, Harish was able to share with Yvette how much pressure he felt from his dad to succeed on the job. Harish's parents immigrated to the U.S. and made huge sacrifices for him to get a good education. He felt torn between pleasing his father and meeting Yvette's needs. Drug use was a way to escape the pain and disengage from feeling pulled in too many directions.

Understanding Harish's family expectations allowed Yvette to see how much pressure Harish was under and unleashed Yvette's compassion. Yvette's newfound ability to be honest and express her true feelings diminished her moodiness and her need to withdraw. When she felt tempted to sulk and turn inward, she pushed herself to speak the truth in love. She knew that a heart-to-heart talk was needed. Yvette also realized that relationships were not as fragile as she feared. Harish valued her honesty. Eventually she was able to shed the just-be-nice motto.

Over the months they struggled to let go of old patterns, but eventually Harish trimmed his work hours down to a manageable amount and found other ways to deal with his stress. Mountain biking with his buddies and downloading relaxing music to his iPod enabled him to give up smoking weed. The problems that erupted in their dating relationship were God's way of getting them to deal with areas of brokenness. Today Harish and Yvette are married and love each other deeply.

DISCERNING INCOMPATIBILITIES

Leanne and I met in a coffee shop, where she shared that she was having major doubts about her relationship with Sherman. Their problems seemed to center on togetherness versus independence. Leanne often felt smothered by Sherman's frequent desire to be together. Sherman felt blown off by Leanne who often chose to spend time jogging alone or with her girlfriends instead of being with him. This same issue of togetherness and independence seemed to surface weekly. Leanne often had a nagging feeling that she was disappointing Sherman, yet she also felt annoyed by his excessive desire to be together.

Leanne came from a family that valued autonomy and career development. A sign of love in her family was to give each other a long leash. Her mom lived out of state away from the family for two years during Leanne's high school years to attend school. The family applauded her dad's support and sacrifice that enabled her mom to pursue her career dreams.

Sherman on the other hand, was from a tight-knit family. His dad was a pastor and his mom didn't work outside the home, so family life revolved around the church. Grocery shopping, ministry, work and cooking were shared by his parents.

I drew a continuum for Leanne:

---

togetherness/enmeshed   autonomy/disconnected

I asked Leanne to put an LP (for Leanne's parents) at the point along the continuum where she thought her parents' marriage was and an SP (for Sherman's parents) at the point where she saw Sherman's parents. Then I asked her where she would like to be when she got married and where she thought Sherman would like to be.

Leanne's parents were way to the right and Sherman's parents were way to the left. She put herself closer to the center than her parents, but near the autonomy end. She put Sherman pretty near his parents.

SP	S		L	LP

togetherness/enmeshed   autonomy/disconnected

The gulf between their families was striking. Somehow seeing the continuum in black and white helped explain why they were so conflicted over the question of togetherness. Leanne realized they were both reenacting their family values. No wonder they had major clashes.

I asked Leanne, "Imagine that you and Sherman broke up. Imagine that he met a wonderful woman and was happy and planned to marry her. Let that scenario form in your mind. How do you feel?"

Leanne sat for a moment and then said, "Relieved."

"Really, you wouldn't feel jealous?"

She said, "No, I honestly would feel relieved." She realized she wanted a way out but didn't want to hurt Sherman.

Asking yourself that same question can uncover your true feelings. If you feel relieved, let off the hook or set free, chances are you need to break up.

The next weekend Leanne told Sherman about her perception of their incompatibilities and her sense that they should break up. He was initially hurt and asked, "Is there someone else? Did I do something wrong?" Leanne assured him neither was the case. Over time Sherman reluctantly agreed they weren't a match. Sadness set in as they both grieved the death of a dream, a dream of life together. But in their heart of hearts, they knew it was the right choice.

Sherman and Leanne are a good example of two wonderful people who simply aren't compatible. Neither one is wrong or bad, they just don't seem to be a match. This can be hard to face, especially when the person you're dating has so many desirable and admirable traits.

MAKING THE BREAK

It can be extremely difficult to come to the conclusion that you need to break up. It may feel more comfortable and even safer to stay in the relationship. However, it can be damaging to stay in a dating relationship with an eye toward upgrading when someone better comes along. We can be so hungry for companionship and the need to feel special that dating can become an addiction. If you find that you're *always* in a dating relationship, sometimes dating people you know you would never marry, ask yourself why.

What about the situation in which a couple has been dating for several years and the relationship is in a holding pattern? Perhaps one person wants to move forward toward marriage and the other person is content to date.

Some people have difficulty making a commitment because the enormity of marriage immobilizes them. If this is your situation, or that of the person you're dating, it might be helpful to get input from a trusted friend, counselor or pastor. That person can help you probe for the reasons you seem stuck and help you determine if this inability to commit is demonstrated in other areas of your life.

Taking a significant break, perhaps a few months, with no communication between you, and spending time in prayer seeking the Lord's leading may be helpful. Separation may make the reluctant person realize how much he or she misses the partner. Or the time apart may be liberating.

If you're dating someone who is averse to commitment, you may want to decide how long you'll continue to date without becoming engaged. I have seen people give away years of their lives hoping for their significant others to make a commitment. The length of time you choose may depend on your life stage. A 23-year-old person may be willing to date with no commitment for a longer time than a 32-year-old person.

ASKING GOD TO LEAD

As you consider the decision of whether to break up, ask God to guide you. Are the problems in your relationship traits God may want to change? Are there areas of brokenness that God may want to heal? Is God leading you to work on your issues or is God leading you to break up? Also, seek the counsel of trusted friends, your pastor, your siblings and your parents or other older adults. Often people outside the relationship see things you might be blind to.

God leads people to get married, but God also leads people to break up. If it's the latter, do it face to face, not on the phone or in writing. This decreases the likelihood of miscommunication or misunderstanding. Choose a time and place that allows you to have a good heart-to-heart conversation. You don't want to be rushed or interrupted. Keep in mind that you want to part company with a minimum of pain. Choose to act with integrity by your words and actions even in the breakup process.

After you break up with a person decide not to date anyone for a month or two. Even if you have feelings for a new person, put that on hold. Jumping from one person to another too quickly doesn't give you time to adequately autopsy your former relationship. You need to take some time to figure out what went wrong and what you can learn from the experience. Dating someone and breaking up should be a learning experience. Waiting for a season also saves you from the accusation that you were cheating on your former partner.

After your breakup, regardless of who initiated, you may be challenged to let go of the connection you feel toward your ex. Sexual activity (including kissing and cuddling) causes two people to bond. While this is a great thing in marriage, it's a negative thing when you're trying to break up. Also, sharing intimately can leave you feeling bonded to your former partner. Even when communication has been clear and you have officially broken up, getting your heart to catch up is hard.

Many people have found it helpful to pray with a trusted friend, a Christian worker or pastor, asking God to help them let go. God has an amazing ability to bind our broken hearts. Choosing to let go and move on allows us to make space in our hearts for God's new plans. One chapter of life is over, but a new chapter begins.

It takes great courage to break up. More than likely, you'll go through a season of pain as you face your aloneness. Many people find that the aloneness they experience is an impetus to depend more fully on Jesus. The words of God "I will never leave you or forsake you" assure us of his sacred friendship that is the constant in our lives. Also, becoming more deeply involved in your faith community can offer you meaningful friendships as you navigate through turbulent times in your romantic life.

34 How can we have a Christ-centered relationship without being cheesy or forced?

Whenever I receive a question like this, I'm greatly encouraged. The fervent desire to make Christ central in a dating relationship is a noble longing. Some have been in destructive dating relationships and want desperately to do things right. For others this desire grows out of a hunger for God and a passion to glorify him in all areas of life.

Most of us have self-doubt and uncertainty about dating and romance in general, but when you add to that confusion about how to make it Christ-centered, people feel clueless. What in the world does that look like?

They imagine a Christ-centered relationship as doing something—praying together or reading the Bible. But a Christ-centered relationship is one that has the presence of Christ permeating every aspect of life, both as individuals and as a couple.

One of the richest texts on Christ-centered relationships is found in Ephesians 4:25–5:3. The apostle Paul spends the first three chapters of Ephesians talking about our wonderful standing in Christ and the spiritual riches that belong to believers. In the last three chapters, he brings this lofty theology down to street level: practical interpersonal relationships in the family, in the marketplace and in other close relationships. Notice the contrasts in which something is to be taken off like a flea-infested garment and something is to be put on like a lovely new sweater.

> Therefore each of you must put off falsehood and speak truthfully to your neighbor, for we are all members of one body. "In your anger do not sin": Do not let the sun go down while you are still angry, and do not give the devil a foothold. Those who have been stealing must steal no longer, but must work, doing something useful with their own hands, that they may have something to share with those in need.
>
> Do not let any unwholesome talk come out of your mouths, but only what is helpful for building others up according to their needs, that it may benefit those who listen. And do not grieve the Holy Spirit of God, with whom you were sealed for the day of redemption. Get rid of all bitterness, rage and anger, brawling and slander, along with every form of malice. Be kind and compassionate to one another, forgiving each other, just as in Christ God forgave you.
>
> Follow God's example, therefore, as dearly loved children and walk in the way of love, just as Christ loved us and gave himself up for us as a fragrant offering and sacrifice to God.
>
> But among you there must not be even a hint of sexual immorality, or of any kind of impurity, or of greed, because these are improper for the Lord's people. (Ephesians 4:25–5:3)

RELATIONAL HONESTY

What can this text teach us about having a Christ-centered dating relationship? The first principle is a call to relational honesty: put off falsehood and speak truthfully. We live in a culture that is permeated with lies. We have become so accustomed to lies that we don't even expect to believe TV commercials, promises from politicians or the boastful exploits of friends. Lying is the cancer of human relationships. It destroys trust, which is essential for any relationship. People often play games in romantic relationships.

Couples seeking to have Christ-centered relationships must push themselves to not fall into any kind of deception. Is there any topic you haven't been honest about? If so, come clean. Resolve that your relationship will be characterized by shooting straight.

The second part, to speak truthfully to our neighbors, is a call to open up and let our partners know what we're thinking and feeling. We must come out from behind our rocks and risk being known. Many dating couples miss out on the intimacy that could be theirs because they don't want their partners to know about the problems they're wrestling with. Pride and the need to be seen as having it all together creates isolation.

If a woman is dealing with an eating disorder but can't bring herself to tell the guy she's dating about it, it creates a relational barrier. If a man is experiencing failure on the job but can't bring himself to talk about his fear of being fired, it creates relational distance.

I encourage you to be transparent, to open up and have heart-to-heart talks. To be known and loved is powerful. It gives you confidence to have someone know the real you and still be loved. By opening up, you allow your partner to be God's love with skin on. Your relationship moves toward a deeper level of intimacy.

On a related topic, the Ephesians text assumes we'll be angry: "In your anger do not sin." So keep short accounts by dealing with it by sundown. If we don't deal with anger quickly and constructively, we give the devil a foothold. Some people come from homes where anger is repressed; issues are denied and buried. Other people come from homes where anger is explosively expressed; people lash out and become verbally or physically hurtful. Talk with your partner about how anger was dealt with growing up. What was good? What was bad? As you form a Christ-centered relationship, you can learn constructive ways to deal with anger as a couple.

RELATIONSHIP SENSITIVITY

The second principle is a call to relationship sensitivity. Read verse 29 again: "Do not let any unwholesome talk come out of your mouths, but only what is helpful for building others up according to their needs, that it may benefit those who listen." Honesty in dating does not mean that we blurt out everything we think. We must be honest, but what we say must pass through the filter of being helpful to those who listen. Our words are to build people up, speaking the truth in love.

To have a Christ-centered relationship, you may have to have some hard conversations. You need to learn to communicate in ways that benefit your partner. Before you talk about a sensitive issue, ask yourself whether your words will be helpful to your partner and whether he or she will be built up by them.

RELATIONAL HEALING

The third principle is a call to relational healing. We're to forsake damaging ways of relating like bitterness, rage, anger and brawling. It's hard to believe this was written to Christians. As we discard harmful behaviors we're to put on kindness, compassion and forgiveness (verse 32).

A Christ-centered relationship should be characterized by kindness and compassion. Kindness might mean driving miles out of your way to pick up your partner after work. It might mean running to the store for medications when he's sick or for computer paper so she can make a deadline. Compassion moves beyond feelings and propels you to enter into the concerns of the person you're dating.

That may mean being understanding if past sexual abuse makes your partner uneasy with certain kinds of touch.

To forgive each other just as in Christ God forgave you is a tall order. But your own sins and Christ's forgiveness of you provides a backdrop for seeing your partner's sins. The ability to forgive is one more characteristic of a Christ-centered relationship.

Relationships that keep a scorecard of wrongs eventually grow cold. A long-term relationship alive with love is only possible between people who know how to forgive. As imperfect human beings, we *will* screw up. Learning to apologize and ask for forgiveness and also to give it is so necessary.

RELATIONAL PURITY

The last section of this passage is a call to relational purity. "But among you there must not be even a hint of sexual immorality, or of any kind of impurity, or of greed, because these are improper for God's holy people." A Christ-centered dating relationship will be characterized by purity and chastity. This rests on the belief that sex is one of God's good gifts, a precious gift to be enjoyed in God's timing and in God's ways. Restrictions are viewed as God's loving care for his people.

In this stage of building a Christ-centered dating relationship, time and energy can be poured into developing a deep friendship with one another and learning how to convey love apart from physical involvement. Time and energy can also be directed outward in the service of others, practicing hospitality, doing volunteer work, coaching a kids' sports team or taking a dance class together.

Even though certain activities like prayer, Bible study and attending church are not add-ons that make a dating relationship Christ-centered, they do have spiritual benefits and should be a part of a dating couple's experience. Attending church together and discussing the sermon or teaching children's Sunday school together or helping with yard cleanup day together, can be valuable as you learn what it means to be part of a larger faith community and try your hand at ministering and serving as a team.

It's also beneficial to spend time with married Christian couples who can serve as role models and mentors. Seeing Christ in their relationship and how faith is lived out in the context of marriage will help you form ideas.

A Christ-centered dating relationship grows out of two individuals who keep their own spiritual fires burning. Each member of the dating couple needs to make sure to be vitally connected to Christ and growing in their individual relationship with the Lord. If the only time you pray or read the Bible is with your partner, you may be spiritually dependent on that person and not on God. One of the great challenges is to prevent the person you're dating from replacing God in your life.

A dating relationship centered on Christ is radically countercultural. You'll find yourself out of step with mainstream society in the realm of romance. Perhaps there is no other area of life that marks you as a Christian more than your pursuit of love relationships. People will watch and say, "I see Christ in your relationship," because they see a compelling picture of love that's honest, faithful, sacrificial and pure. Your personal rewards will be great, and you'll shine forth the light of Christ to a watching world.

Epilogue

When my oldest child, Tiffany, was about two years old she became very ill. Her little stomach was so agitated that she couldn't keep anything down. As a new mom, inexperienced with sick toddlers, I called our pediatrician. Even though she kept saying she was hungry, the doctor instructed me to give her nothing at all for two hours so her stomach could settle down. Even if she begged for food, I was to give her absolutely nothing.

After I got off the phone, Tiffany kept following me around, tugging on my shirt and saying, "Hungy. I hungy, Mommy. I eat." I did my best to explain to her that for a little while she couldn't eat anything until her stomach settled down. But I am afraid her two-year-old understanding was insufficient. It was heart-wrenching to turn a deaf ear to her mournful pleas, but I knew it was for her best. She finally gave up.

A little while later, I noticed Tiffany stooping down by the refrigerator. Her tiny hand with her teeny fingers reached under the refrigerator to pick up a dusty Cheerio. As she drew the dusty Cheerio up to her mouth, I stepped in with one great swoop and intercepted the Cheerio. Her big blue eyes looked up at me. She stared in disbelief. She couldn't believe that I would take this morsel away from her.

I said to her, "Tiffany, I have to take this dusty Cheerio away from you. Right now, you can't eat anything. I have food for you, and I'll give you a feast when the time is right." Her downcast eyes and frown let me know that she was not convinced.

In that moment, I had a flash of insight. I realized that this little scene in the kitchen was a microcosm of our relationship with God.

We're hungry people, with longings and unmet needs. Like Tiffany, we seek to take matters into our own hands and fulfill our longings with the best we can find. Sometimes we're reaching under the refrigerator for a dusty Cheerio because it's all we can see.

How hard it is to live with unmet longings, to hold out, to wait, to believe God will supply our needs in his way, in his time.

This is often true in our romantic relationships. We latch on to the best we can find at the time, unwilling to hold out for God's best. One of the challenges of the Christian faith is finding the grace to live with unfulfilled longings. My prayer for you is that your unmet longings will draw you more deeply into the presence of God. That you would seek God's will for you in your love life and every other aspect. Only in heaven will all of our longings be met.

I hope this book has given you some helpful ideas about how to pursue romantic relationships in a way that honors God and values his gift of sex through a life of integrity, purity and healthy relationships.

Don't settle for dusty Cheerios. God wants to give you a feast, if you will only wait for him to unfold his plans.

Notes

Part 1: Sex

[1]Philip Yancey, *Designer Sex* (Downers Grove, Ill.: InterVarsity Press, 2005), p. 29.

[2]Lisa McMinn, *Sexuality and Holy Longing* (San Francisco: Jossey-Bass, 2004), p. 55.

[3]Robbie Castleman, *True Love in a World of False Hope* (Downers Grove, Ill.: Inter-Varsity Press, 1996), p. 93.

[4]Henry Cloud and John Townsend, *Boundaries* (Grand Rapids: Zondervan, 1992).

[5]Roxanne Roberts, "Jilted Bride Writes an Etiquette Guide for the Nearly Wed," *Pittsburgh Post-Gazette,* 7 August 2003, Lifestyle section <www.post-gazette.com/lifestyle/20030807nearlywedl3.asp>.

[6]Laura Sessions Stepp, "Study: Half of All Teens Have Had Oral Sex," *Washington Post,* 16 September 2005, p. A07.

[7]One author put the generational difference this way, "'We [the older generation] used to talk about sex in terms of first base, second base and so on. Oral sex was maybe in the dugout.' The news for parents, he [Bill Albert, communications director for the National Campaign to Prevent Teen Pregnancy] said, is that they must broaden the discussions they have with their children about sex and be more specific. 'If they want their teens to abstain from sex, they need to say exactly what they want their kids to abstain from'" (ibid.).

[8]John Hall, "Study Suggests Most Teens Break Abstinence Pledges," *American Baptist Press,* December 4, 2003 <www.abpnews.com/2528.article>.

[9]Claire Brindis, quoted in Stepp, "Study: Half of All Teens," p. A07.

[10]Gary Chapman, *The Five Love Languages* (Chicago: Northfield, 1995), p. 38.

[11]Ramona Richards, "Dirty Little Secret," *Today's Christian Woman* 25, no. 5 (September/October 2003): 58 <www.christianitytoday.com/tcw/2003/sepoct/5.58.html>.

[12]A helpful resource for turning away from pornography is Mark Laaser's study guide *Faithful and True, Sexual Integrity in a Fallen World* (Nashville: LifeWay, 1996). Countless men have been set free by using this study guide and opening up to others in their small groups about their struggles.

A book that offers hope to women who struggle with pornography and other sexual addictions is *Nice Girls Don't: An Honest Look at Female Sexual Addiction* by Wendy Eaton (Downers Grove, Ill.: InterVarsity Press, forthcoming).

Websites that offer help to men and women struggling with addiction to pornography are <www.settingcaptivesfree.com>, <www.purelifeministries.org> and <www.pureonline.com>.

[13]C. S. Lewis to Mr. Mason, March 6, 1956, as quoted in Leanne Payne, *The Broken Image: Restoring Personal Wholeness Through Healing Prayer* (Wheaton, Ill.: Crossway, 1981).

[14]McMinn, *Sexuality and Holy Longing*, p. 62.

[15]Michelle Graham, *Wanting to Be Her: Body Image Secrets Victoria Won't Tell You* (Downers Grove, Ill.: InterVarsity Press, 2005), pp. 104-5.

[16]Yancey, *Designer Sex*, pp. 12-13.

[17]Mary Ellen Ashcroft, *Temptations Women Face* (Downers Grove, Ill.: InterVarsity Press, 1993), p. 133.

[18]Archibald Hart, Catherine Hart Webber and Debra Taylor, *Secrets of Eve: Understanding the Meaning of Female Sexuality* (Nashville: Word Publishing, 1998), p. 181.

[19]Kathleen, *Healing from Sexual Abuse* (Downers Grove, Ill: InterVarsity Press, 1999), pp. 10-11.

[20]Wendy Maltz, *Sexual Healing Journey* (New York: Harper Perennial, 1991), pp. 85-107, cited in Hart, *Secrets of Eve*, p. 197.

[21]Sandra D. Wilson, *Released from Shame* (Downers Grove, Ill.: InterVarsity Press, 1990); Kathleen, *Healing from Sexual Abuse;* Ruth Goring, *Date Rape* (Downers Grove, Ill.: InterVarsity Press, 1996).

[22]Natural anesthetics, such as henbane and opiates, had been used by women since antiquity to ease the pain of childbirth, but later the church forbade them (Stan Gundry, *Woman Be Free!* [Grand Rapids: Zondervan, 1977], p. 48).

Eufame MacLayne was tried in Scotland in 1591 for hiring a midwife to provide her with "a certain medicine for the relief of pain in childbirth contrary to Divine law and in contempt of the Crown." She gave birth to twins who were taken from her and she was burned to death for her offense (Bernard Seeman, *Man Against Pain* [Philadelphia: Chilton, 1962], p. 96).

Almost three hundred years later in 1847 an article was published in an Edinburgh medical journal protesting the use of pain-alleviating medications for women in labor appealing to the divine order that "in pain she shall bring forth children" (Seeman, *Man Against Pain*, p. 123). It seems insanely cruel to forbid women the use of painkillers in childbirth, but this was motivated by a desire to uphold the Word of God. Today's enlightened church freely permits women to use medication in childbirth, and most people are unaware that this was ever an area of theological debate.

[23]Stanton L. Jones, *The Gay Debate* (Downers Grove, Ill.: InterVarsity Press, 1994), p. 15.

[24]Amy Orr-Ewing, *Is the Bible Intolerant?* (Downers Grove, Ill.: InterVarsity Press, 2005), p. 120.

[25]Ibid., pp. 120-21.

[26]Lauren F. Winner, *Real Sex* (Grand Rapids: Brazos, 2005), pp. 89-90.

[27]Benoit Denizet-Lewis, "Friends, Friends with Benefits and the Benefits of the Local Mall," *New York Times,* May 30, 2004.

[28]Mike Yaconelli, *Messy Spirituality,* (Grand Rapids: Zondervan, 2002), p. 13.

Part 2: Dating

[1]Joshua Harris, *I Kissed Dating Goodbye* (Sisters, Ore.: Multnomah Publishers, 1997).

[2]With these real concerns in mind, other books were spawned that advocated courtship, betrothal and arranged marriages. If you're interested in learning more about the many Christian views of finding a marriage partner, check out the book, *Five Paths to the Love of your Life,* edited by Alex Chediak (Colorado Springs: NavPress, 2005). Several authors, who all believe in the trustworthiness of the Bible, set forth their differing views on how to find a marriage partner in a God-honoring way. Two of the contributing authors are Jeramy Clark, author of *I Gave Dating a Chance* (Colorado Springs: Waterbrook, 2000), a response to Joshua Harris's book, and his wife, Jerusha Clark.

[3]*Time* magazine published an interesting article about the surprising new research that reveals the profound influence our siblings have on us: Jeff Kluger, "The New Science of Siblings," *Time,* July 10, 2006, pp. 46-55.

[4]Masumi Toyotome, *Three Kinds of Love* (Downers Grove, Ill.: InterVarsity Press, 1961), pp. 12-13.

[5]Mike Mason, *The Mystery of Marriage* (Portland, Ore.: Multnomah Press, 2001), pp. 59-60.

[6]Paul Little, *Affirming the Will of God* (Downers Grove, Ill.: InterVarsity Press, 2001), pp. 4, 7-8.

[7]You may also consider using the *Prepare Inventory,* developed by the University of Minnesota, which examines relationship strengths and growth areas. Over two million couples have used this inventory since its inception in 1980. You can find

counselors and clergy in your hometown at the website, <www.prepare-enrich.com>, to administer this inventory and help you understand the results. Another great resource is Should *I Get Married?* by Blaine M Smith (Downers Grove, Ill.: InterVarsity Press, 2000).

[8]C. S. Lewis, *The Problem of Pain* (New York: Macmillan, 1977), p. 93.

[9]Lewis Smedes, "Forgiveness: The Power to Change the Past," *Christianity Today* (January 7, 1983), p. 24.

[10]C. S. Lewis, *The Four Loves* (Orlando: Harcourt, 1988), p. 121.

[11]Joel Warne, *The Intimate Journey* (Plymouth, Minn.: WellSpring Life Resources), p. 2, 4.

[12]Henry Cloud, *How to Get a Date Worth Keeping* (Grand Rapids: Zondervan, 2005), p. 61.

[13]Ibid., p. 38.

[14]Ibid., p. 37.

[15]The National Marriage Project, David Popenoe and Barbara Dafoe Whitehead (2000), Rutgers, The State University of New Jersey, "Should We Live Together?: What Young Adults Need to Know About Cohabitation Before Marriage" <http://marriage.rutgers.edu/Publications/SWLT2%20TEXT.htm>.

[16]Ibid.

[17]Pamela Smock, *Annual Reviews Sociology* 26, no. 584 (2000): 1-20.

[18]Ibid.

[19]Diane Swanbrow, "Living Together: Sociologist Studies Facts, Myths About 'Living in Sin,'" *The University Record* (University of Michigan), February 14, 2000 <www.umich.edu/~urecord/9900/Feb14_00/6.htm>.

[20]Susan L. Brown, "The Effect of Union Type on Psychological Well-Being: Depression among Cohabitors versus Marrieds," *Journal of Health and Social Behavior* 41, no. 2 (2000).

[21]Todd K. Shackelford, "Cohabitation, Marriage and Murder," *Aggressive Behavior* 27 (2001): 284-91.

[22]Andrew J Cherlin, Kathleen E. Kiernan, and P. Lindsay Chase-Lansdale, "Parental Divorce in Childhood and Demographic Outcomes in Young Adulthood," *Demography* 32, no. 3 (1995): 299-318.

[23]Mason, *Mystery of Marriage,* p. 91.

[24]A groundbreaking book has been written about the benefits of being married: *The Case for Marriage: Why Married People Are Happier, Healthier, and Better Off Financially,* by Linda Waite and Maggie Gallagher (New York: Doubleday, 2000). The book flap says, "Everyone knows that we are experiencing an epidemic of divorce;

rates of single-parenthood and unmarried cohabitation are skyrocketing while marriage rates continue to decline. Yet 93% of Americans still say they hope to form a lasting and happy union with one person, though fewer now believe that this is possible.

"Numerous books have been written about the impact of divorce on men, women, children, and society at large. But no one has yet studied the long-term benefits of being and staying married. The Case for Marriage is a critically important intervention in the national debate about the future of the family. Based on the authoritative research of family sociologist Linda Waite and other scholars, the book's findings dramatically contradict the anti-marriage myths that have become the common sense of most Americans.

"Today a broad consensus holds that marriage is a bad deal for women, that divorce is better for children when parents are unhappy, and that marriage is essentially a private choice, not a public institution. Waite and Gallagher flatly contradict these assumptions, arguing instead that by a broad range of indices, being married is actually better for you physically, materially, and spiritually than being single or divorced. Married people live longer, have better health, earn more money and accumulate more wealth, feel more fulfilled in their lives, enjoy more satisfying sexual relationships and have happier and more successful children than those who remain single, cohabit or get divorced."

These sociological studies confirm the wisdom of God's plan. When we follow the guidelines laid out in the Bible, the outcome is wellness and wholeness.

[25]Mason, Mystery of Marriage, p. 139.

[26]Joachim Jeremias, Jerusalem in the Time of Jesus (Minneapolis: Augsburg Fortress, 1979).